D0512738

Books should be retur...

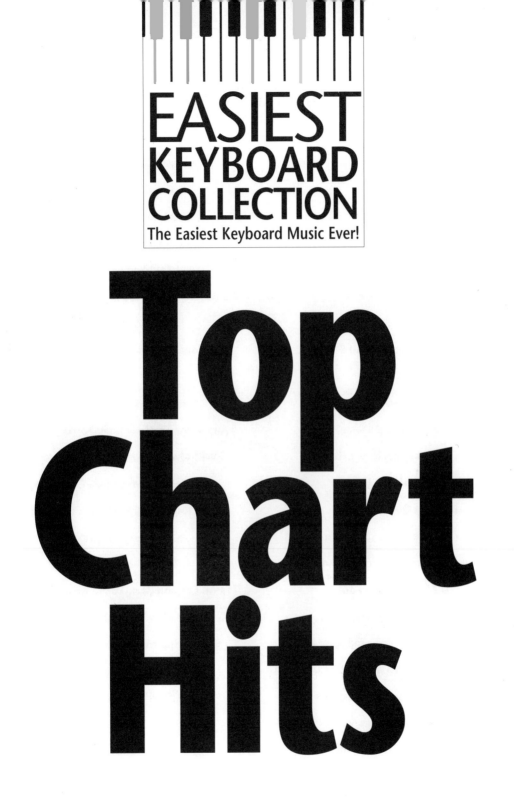

EASIEST KEYBOARD COLLECTION
The Easiest Keyboard Music Ever!

Top Chart Hits

Wise Publications/Omnibus Press
London/New York/Paris/Sydney/Copenhagen/Madrid/Tokyo

Contents

AIN'T NOBODY

Words & Music by David Wolinski
© Copyright 1983 Windswept Pacific Music d/b/a Full Keel Music Company, USA.
EMI Music Publishing (WP) Limited, 127 Charing Cross Road, London WC2.
All Rights Reserved. International Copyright Secured.

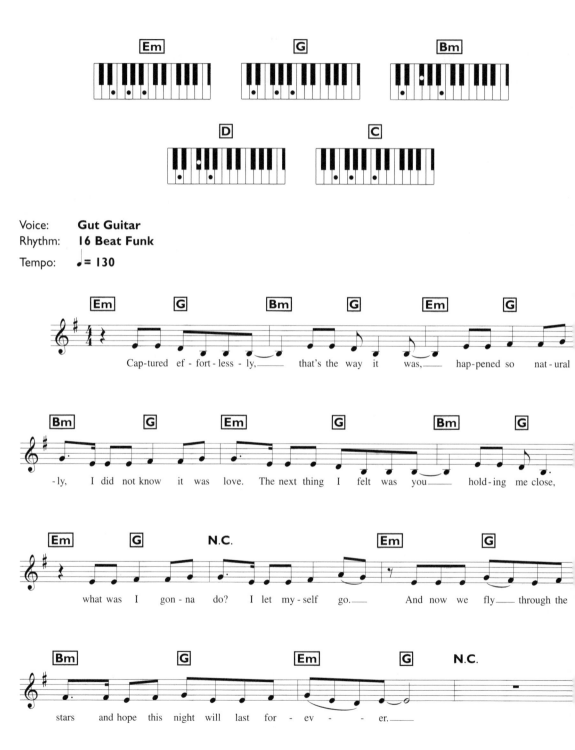

Voice: **Gut Guitar**
Rhythm: **16 Beat Funk**
Tempo: ♩ = 130

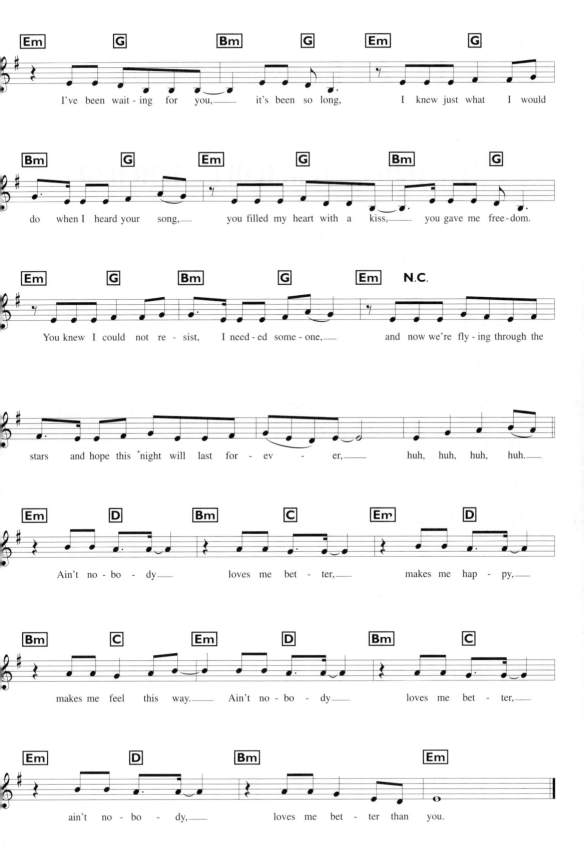

ALWAYS

Words & Music by Jon Bon Jovi

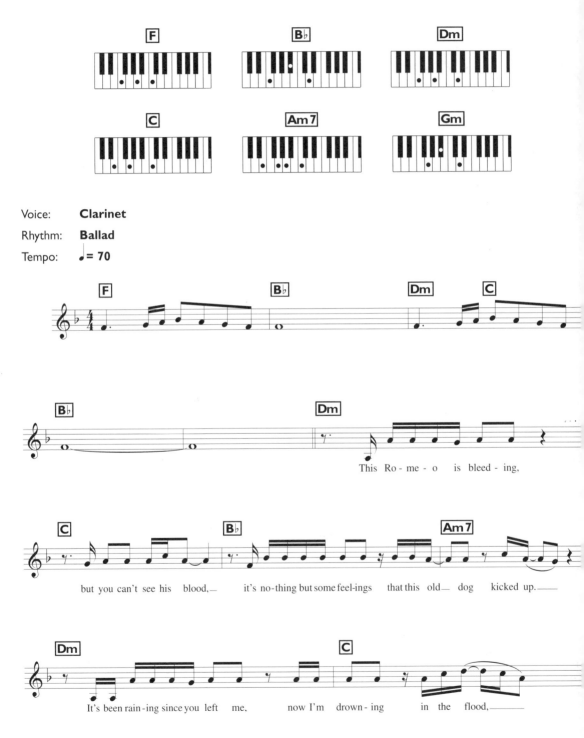

Voice: **Clarinet**

Rhythm: **Ballad**

Tempo: ♩ **= 70**

This Ro-me-o is bleed-ing, but you can't see his blood,— it's no-thing but some feel-ings that this old— dog kicked up.—

It's been rain-ing since you left me, now I'm drown-ing in the flood,———

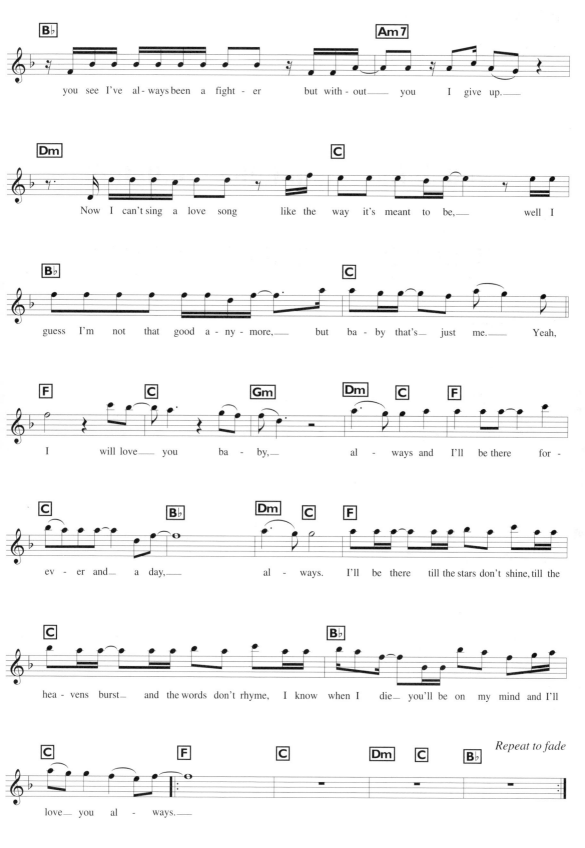

you see I've al-ways been a fight-er but with-out you I give up.

Now I can't sing a love song like the way it's meant to be, well I

guess I'm not that good a-ny-more, but ba-by that's just me. Yeah,

I will love you ba - by, al - ways and I'll be there for -

ev - er and a day, al - ways. I'll be there till the stars don't shine, till the

hea-vens burst and the words don't rhyme, I know when I die you'll be on my mind and I'll

Repeat to fade

love you al - ways.

7

ALWAYS BE MY BABY

Words by Mariah Carey
Music by Jermaine Dupri, Mariah Carey & Manuel Seal

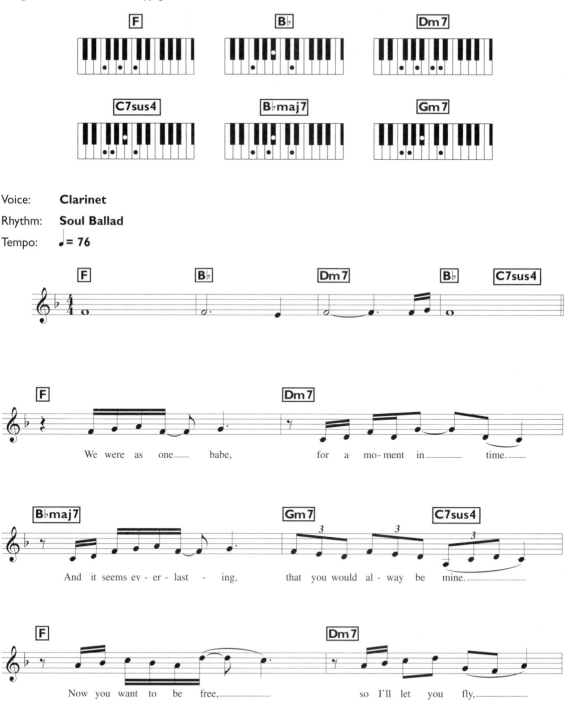

Voice: **Clarinet**

Rhythm: **Soul Ballad**

Tempo: ♩ = 76

We were as one — babe, for a mo-ment in time.

And it seems ev-er-last - ing, that you would al - way be mine.

Now you want to be free, so I'll let you fly,

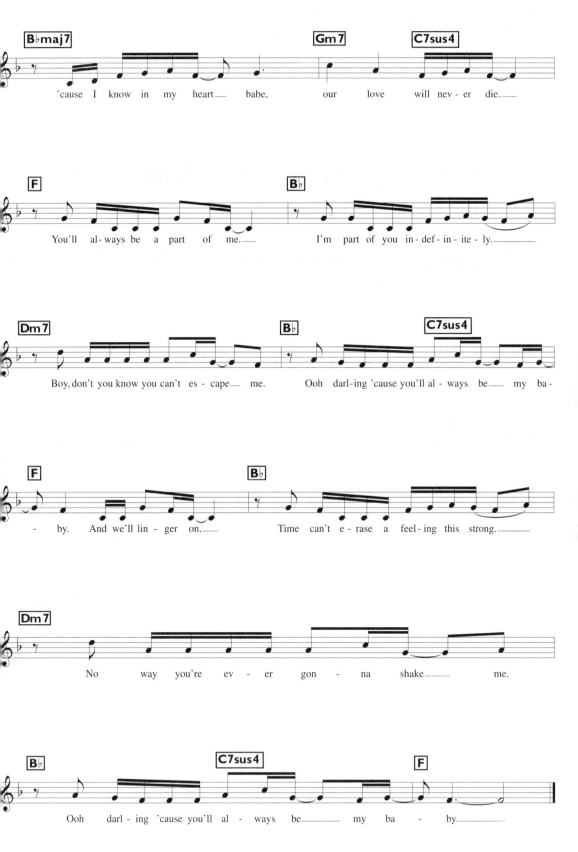

AROUND THE WORLD

Words & Music by Tony Mortimer, Brian Harvey, Matt Rowe & Richard Stannard

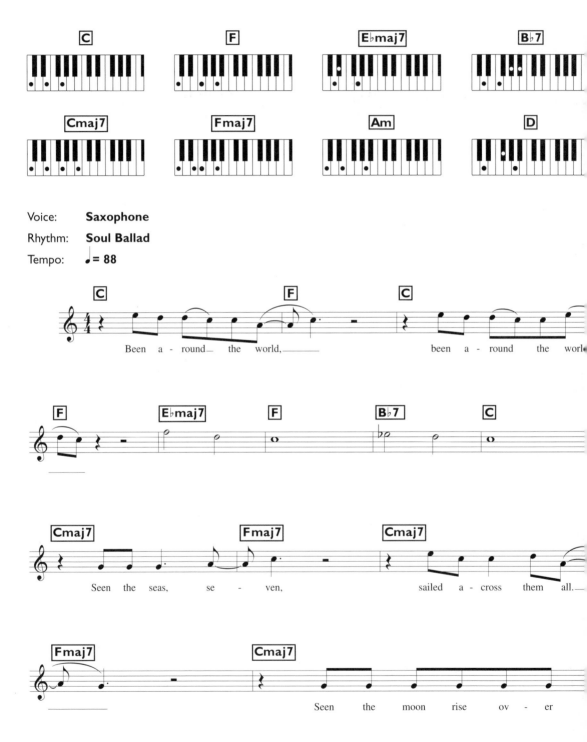

Voice: **Saxophone**

Rhythm: **Soul Ballad**

Tempo: ♩ = 88

Been a - round— the world,_____ been a - round the worl

Seen the seas, se - ven, sailed a - cross them all.

_____ Seen the moon rise ov - er

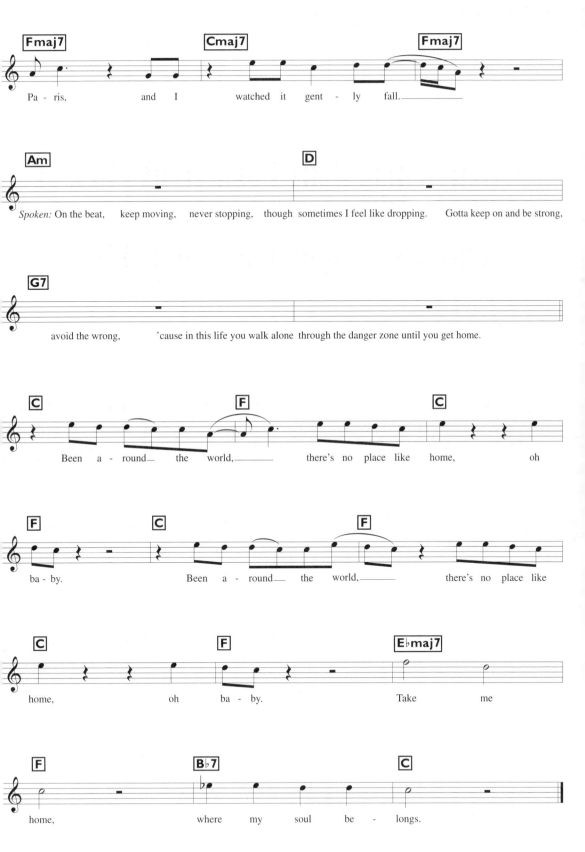

Fmaj7 · Cmaj7 · Fmaj7
Pa - ris, and I watched it gent - ly fall.

Am · D
Spoken: On the beat, keep moving, never stopping, though sometimes I feel like dropping. Gotta keep on and be strong,

G7
avoid the wrong, 'cause in this life you walk alone through the danger zone until you get home.

C · F · C
Been a - round the world, there's no place like home, oh

F · C · F
ba - by. Been a - round the world, there's no place like

C · F · E♭maj7
home, oh ba - by. Take me

F · B♭7 · C
home, where my soul be - longs.

BABY ONE MORE TIME

Words & Music by Max Martin

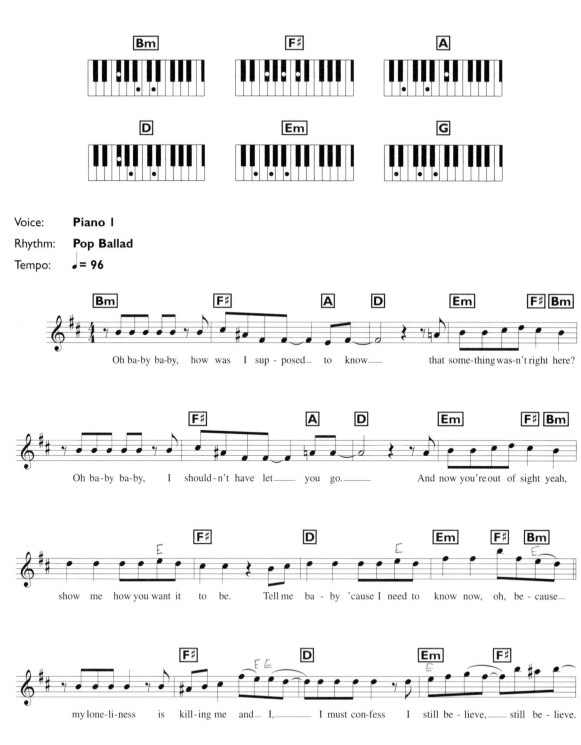

When I'm not with you I lose my mind, give me a sign,—— hit me ba-by one more time.

Oh ba-by ba-by, how was I sup-posed—— to know?——

Oh pret-ty ba-by I should-n't have let—— you go.—— I must con-fess.

—— that my lone-li-ness—— is kill-ing me now.———————— Don't you know I—— still—— be-lieve

—— that you will be here—— and give me a sign.——————— Hit me ba-by one more time.

My lone-li-ness is kill-ing me and—— I,——— I must con-fess I still be-lieve,—— still be-lieve.

Repeat to fade

—— When I'm not with you I lose my mind, give me a sign,—— Hit me ba-by one more time.

BARBIE GIRL

Words & Music by Soren Rasted, Claus Norreen, Rene Dif,
Lene Nystrom, Johnny Pederson & Karsten Delgado

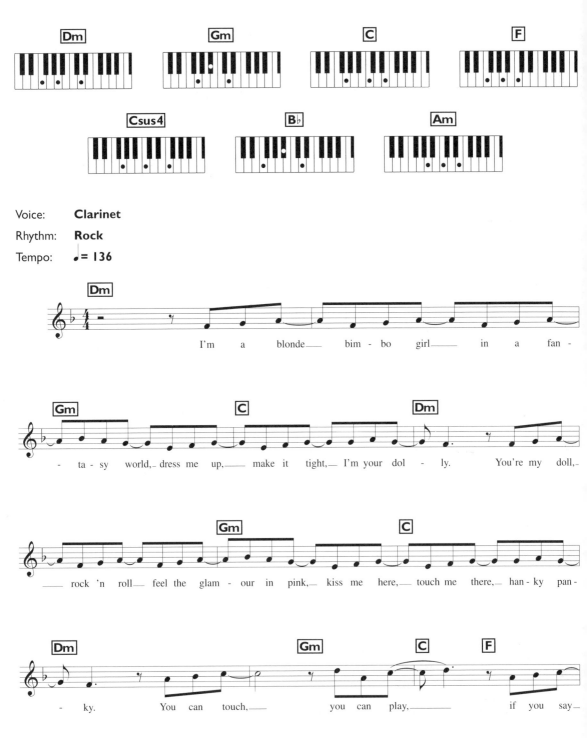

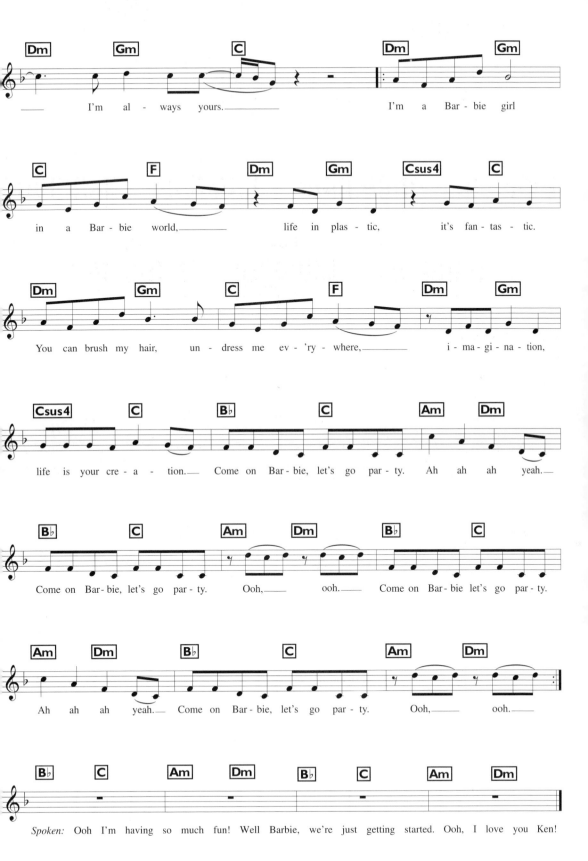

Spoken: Ooh I'm having so much fun! Well Barbie, we're just getting started. Ooh, I love you Ken!

BIG MISTAKE

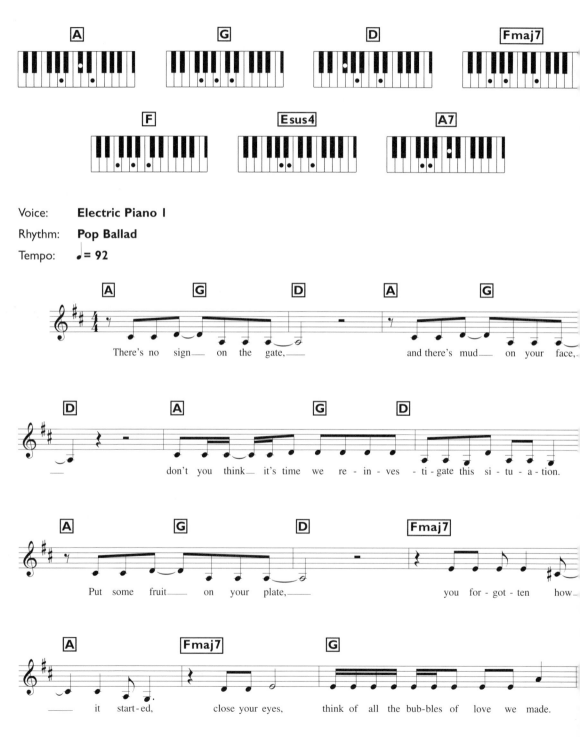

Voice: **Electric Piano 1**

Rhythm: **Pop Ballad**

Tempo: ♩ = 92

There's no sign— on the gate,— and there's mud— on your face,
don't you think— it's time we re-in-ves-ti-gate this si-tu-a-tion.
Put some fruit— on your plate,— you for-got-ten how— it start-ed, close your eyes, think of all the bub-bles of love we made.

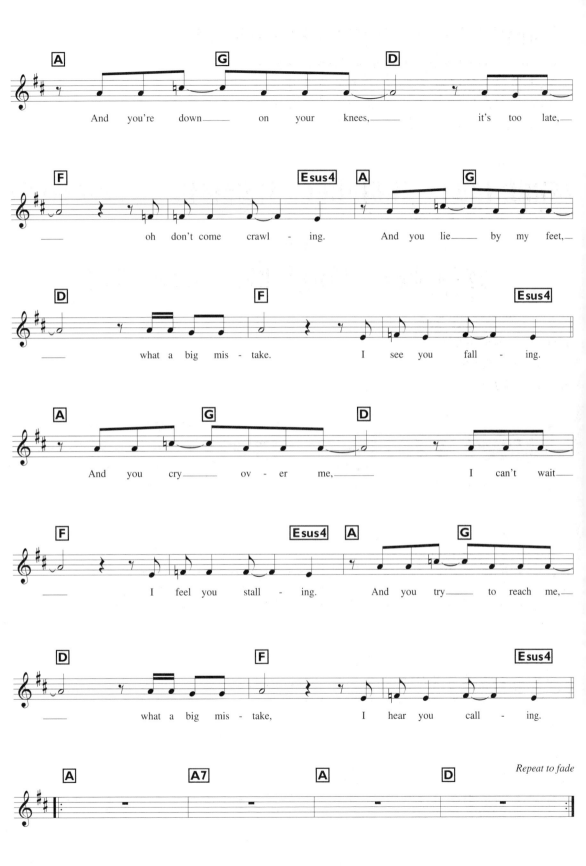

BLAME IT ON THE WEATHERMAN

Words & Music by Ray Hedges, Martin Brannigan, Andy Caine & Tracey Ackerman

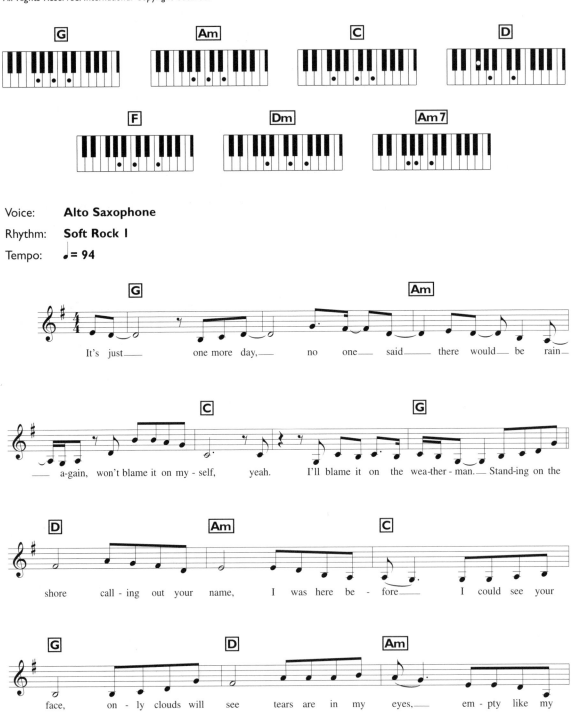

Voice: **Alto Saxophone**

Rhythm: **Soft Rock 1**

Tempo: ♩ = 94

It's just— one more day,— no one— said— there would— be rain—

— a-gain, won't blame it on my - self, yeah. I'll blame it on the wea-ther - man.— Stand-ing on the

shore call - ing out your name, I was here be - fore— I could see your

face, on - ly clouds will see tears are in my eyes, em - pty like my

heart, why d'ya say good - bye?_____ The rain goes

on, on_____ and on a - gain._ The rain goes on, on_____ and

on a - gain._ The rain goes on, on_____ and on a - gain._ May-be it's too late,

may-be it's too late to start a - gain._ May-be I can't pray.

May-be I can't wait, may-be I can't blame the wea-ther - man._ The rain goes

on, on_____ and on a - gain. The rain goes on, on_____ and on a - gain._ The rain goes

on, on_____ and on a - gain._ Oh blame it on the wea-ther - man._

BLINDED BY THE SUN

Words & Music by Chris Helme

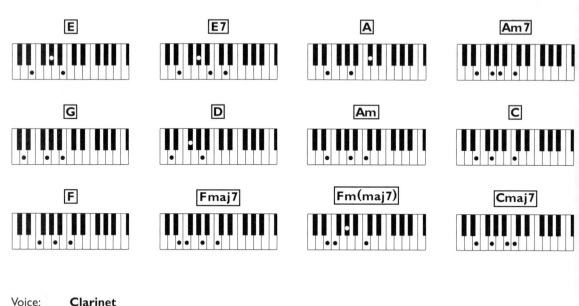

Voice: **Clarinet**

Rhythm: **16 beat**

Tempo: ♩ = 86

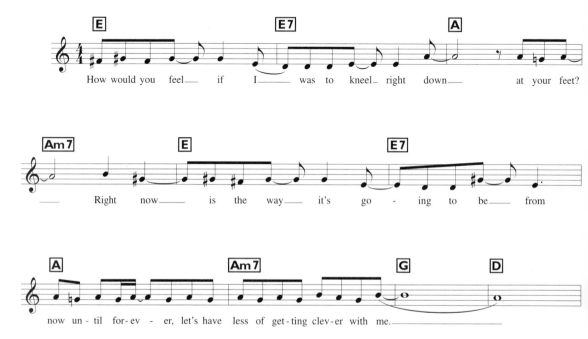

How would you feel____ if I____ was to kneel_ right down____ at your feet?

____ Right now____ is the way____ it's go - ing to be____ from

now un - til for - ev - er, let's have less of get-ting clev-er with me.____

BRING IT ALL BACK

Words & Music by Eliot Kennedy, Mike Percy, Tim Lever & S Club 7
© Copyright 1999 19 Music Limited/BMG Music Publishing Limited,
Bedford House, 69-79 Fulham High Street, London SW6 (53.32%),
Sony/ATV Music Publishing (UK) Limited, 10 Great Marlborough Street, London W1 (26.66%) &
Universal Music Publishing Limited, 77 Fulham Palace Road, London W6 (20.02%).
All Rights Reserved. International Copyright Secured.

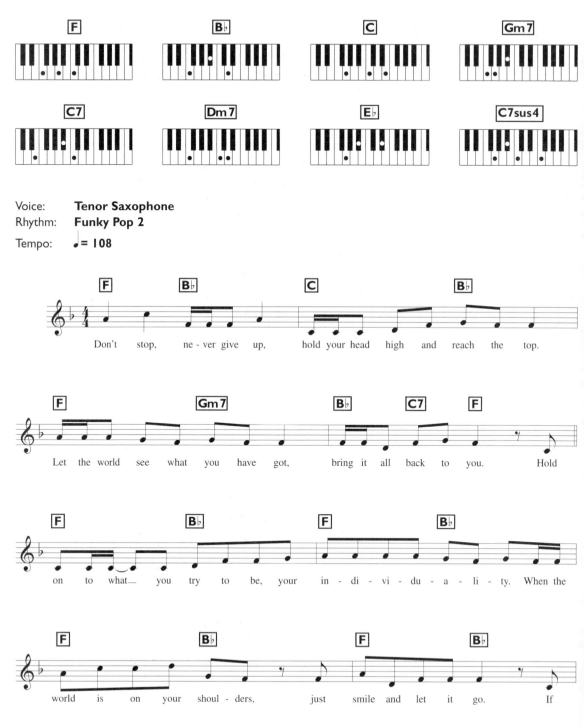

CIRCLE OF LIFE
(From Walt Disney Pictures' "The Lion King")

Music by Elton John
Lyrics by Tim Rice

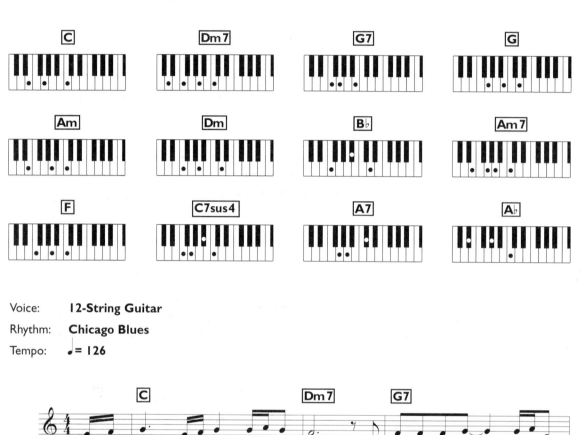

Voice: **12-String Guitar**

Rhythm: **Chicago Blues**

Tempo: ♩ = 126

COMMON PEOPLE

Words by Jarvis Cocker
Music by Pulp

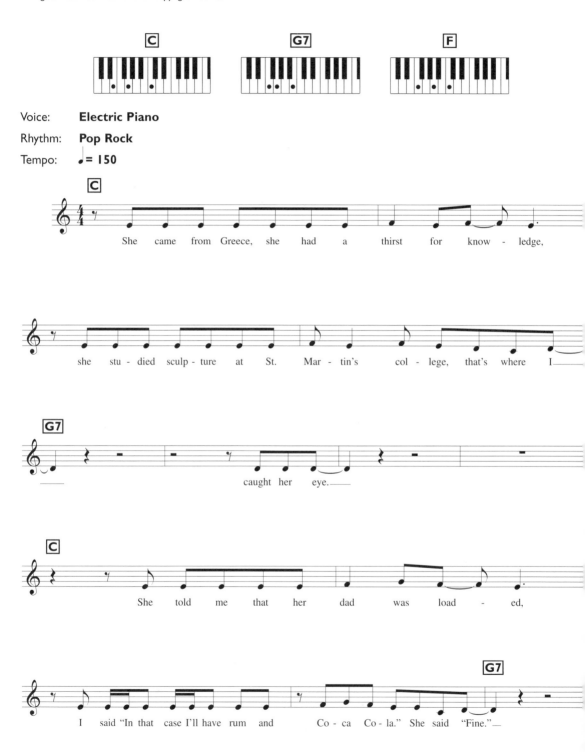

Voice: **Electric Piano**

Rhythm: **Pop Rock**

Tempo: ♩ = 150

And then in thir- ty se- conds time,___ she said

F "I want to live like com- mon peo- ple, I want to do what-

-ev- er com- mon peo- ple do. **C** Want to sleep with

com- mon peo- ple, I want to sleep with com- mon peo- ple like you."

G7 ___ Well what else___ could I do?___ I said I'll...

C I'll see what I can do.

Repeat to fade

Want to live like com- mon peo- ple like you.

COUNTRY HOUSE

Words & Music by Damon Albarn, Graham Coxon,
Alex James & David Rowntree.

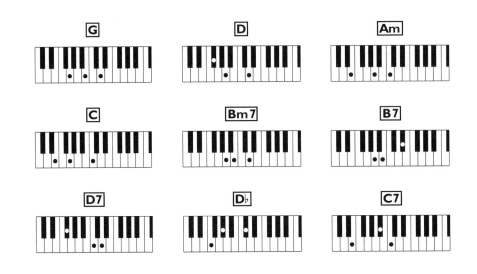

Voice: **Piano**

Rhythm: **Soft Rock**

Tempo: ♩ = 160

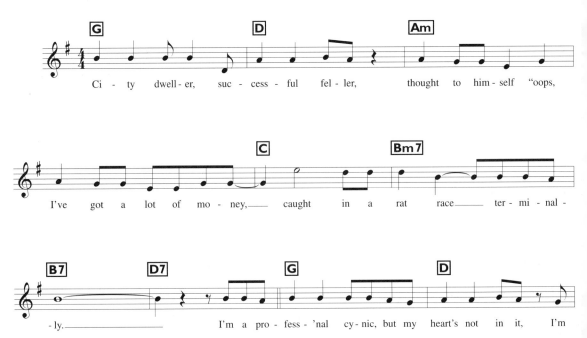

Ci - ty dwell - er, suc - cess - ful fel - ler, thought to him - self "oops,

I've got a lot of mo - ney,— caught in a rat race ter - mi - nal -

- ly.— I'm a pro - fess - 'nal cy - nic, but my heart's not in it, I'm

DANCING QUEEN

Words & Music by Benny Andersson, Björn Ulvaeus & Stig Anderson
© Copyright 1976 Union Songs AB, Stockholm, Sweden for the world.
Bocu Music Limited, I Wyndham Yard, Wyndham Place, London WI for Great Britain and Eire.
All Rights Reserved. International Copyright Secured.

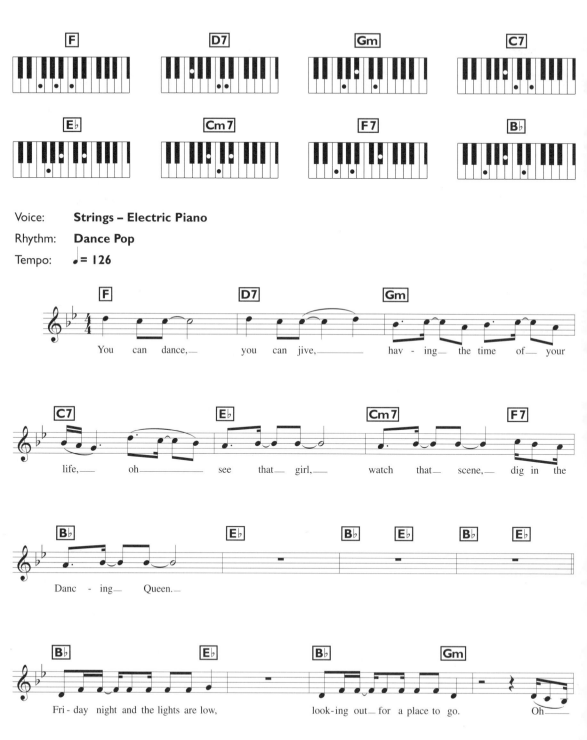

Voice: **Strings – Electric Piano**

Rhythm: **Dance Pop**

Tempo: ♩ = 126

A DESIGN FOR LIFE

Words by Nicky Wire
Music by James Dean Bradfield & Sean Moore

Voice: **Brass Ensemble**

Rhythm: **Slow Rock 1**

Tempo: ♩. = 98

Libraries gave us pow - er, then work came and made us free. What price— now. for— a shal - low piece— of dig - ni - ty. I wish I had a bot - tle— right here in my dir - ty

A DIFFERENT BEAT

Words & Music by Martin Brannigan, Stephen Gately,
Ronan Keating, Shane Lynch, Ray Hedges & Keith Duffy

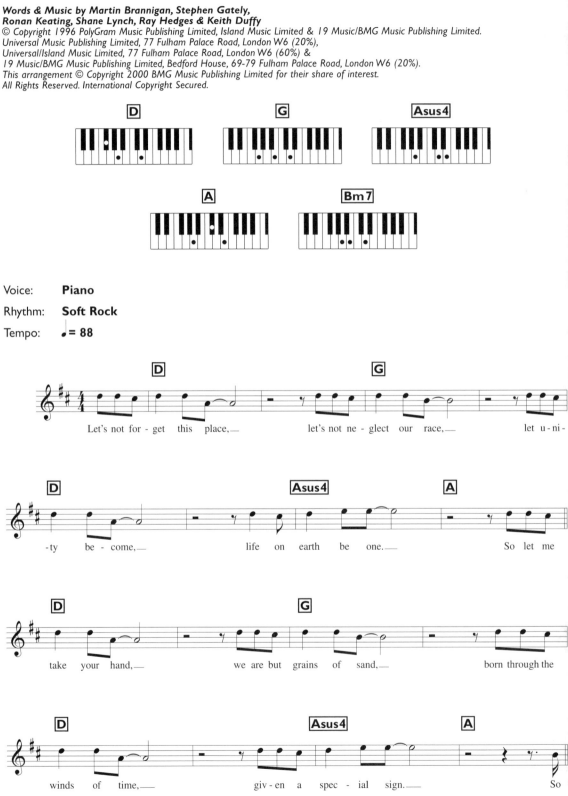

Voice: **Piano**

Rhythm: **Soft Rock**

Tempo: ♩ = 88

Let's not for-get this place,— let's not ne-glect our race,— let u-ni-ty be-come,— life on earth be one.— So let me take your hand,— we are but grains of sand,— born through the winds of time,— giv-en a spec-ial sign.— So

D.I.S.C.O.

Words & Music by Daniel Vangarde & Jean Kluger
© Copyright 1980 Zagora Editions Productions, France.
R & E Music Limited/The International Music Network Limited,
Independent House, 54 Larkshall Road, Chingford, London E4 6PD.

Voice: **Soprano Saxophone**

Rhythm: **Disco**

Tempo: ♩ = 120

ETERNAL FLAME

Words & Music by Billy Steinberg, Tom Kelly & Susanna Hoffs

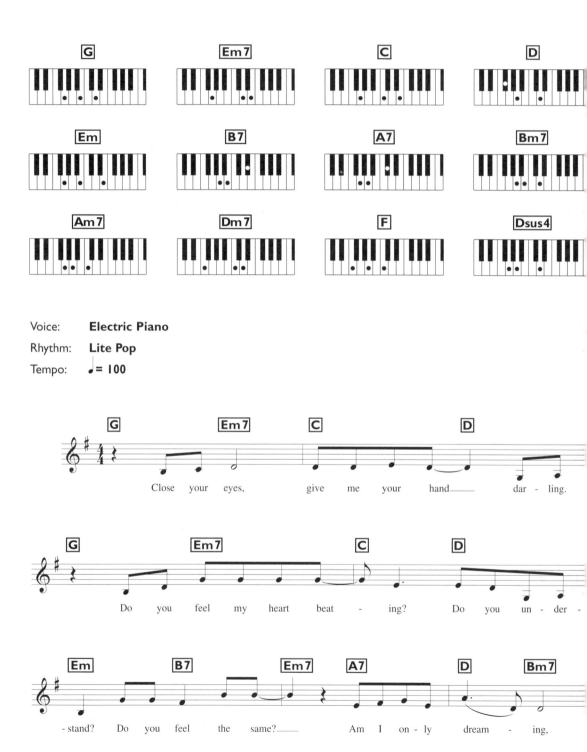

Voice: **Electric Piano**

Rhythm: **Lite Pop**

Tempo: ♩ = 100

Close your eyes, give me your hand darling.

Do you feel my heart beat - ing? Do you un - der -

- stand? Do you feel the same? Am I on - ly dream - ing,

EVERY BREATH YOU TAKE

Words & Music by Sting

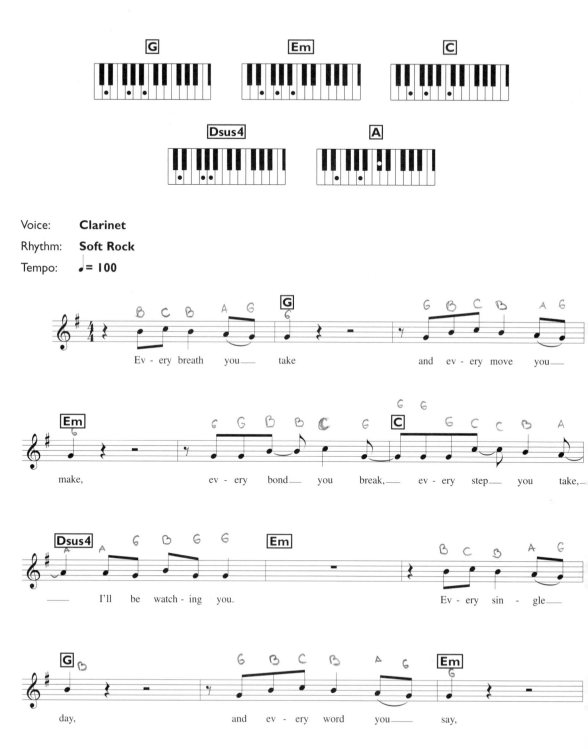

Voice: **Clarinet**

Rhythm: **Soft Rock**

Tempo: ♩ = 100

ev-ery game you play,— ev-ery night you stay,— I'll be watch-ing you.

Oh can't you see, that you be - long to me?

My— poor heart— aches with ev - ery step— you take.

Ev - ery move you— make and ev-ery vow you— break,

ev-ery smile— you fake, ev-ery claim— you stake,— I'll be watch-ing you.

Ev - ery move— you make,— ev-ery step— you take,— I'll be watch-ing you.

Repeat to fade

(EVERYTHING I DO) I DO IT FOR YOU

Words by Bryan Adams & Robert John 'Mutt' Lange
Music by Michael Kamen

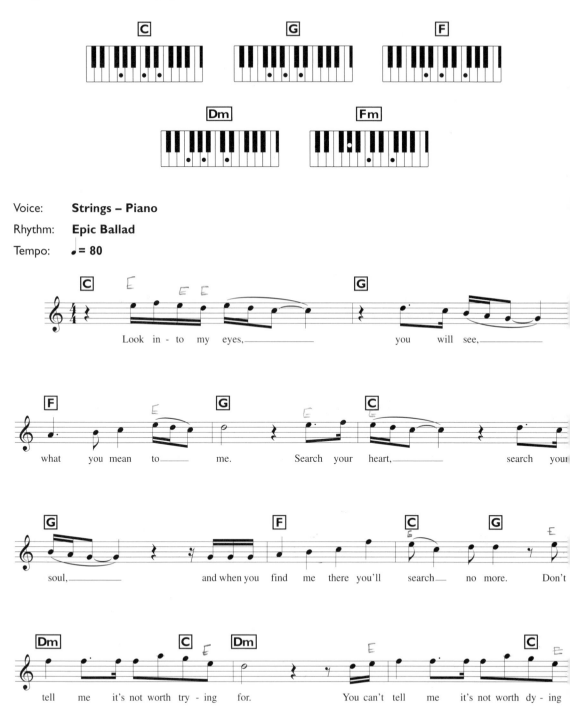

Voice: **Strings – Piano**

Rhythm: **Epic Ballad**

Tempo: ♩ = 80

Look in-to my eyes, you will see,

what you mean to me. Search your heart, search your

soul, and when you find me there you'll search no more. Don't

tell me it's not worth try-ing for. You can't tell me it's not worth dy-ing

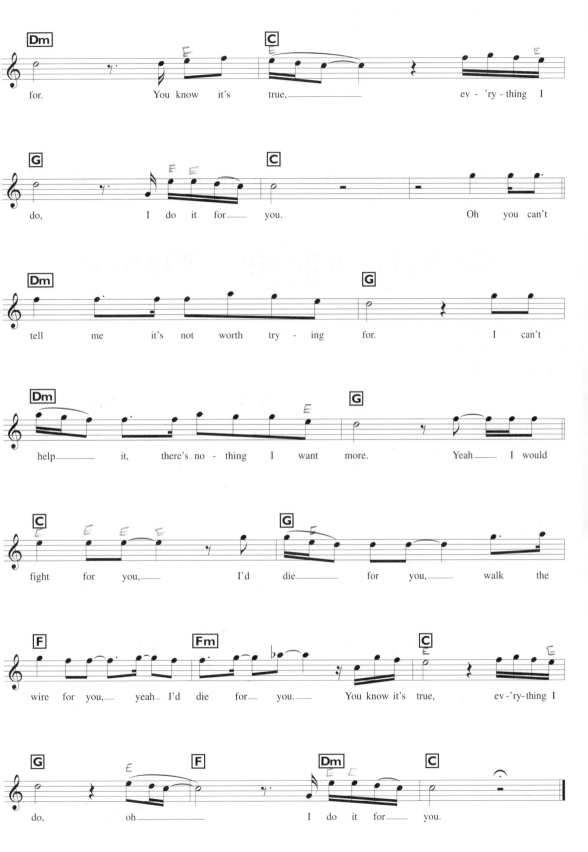

FALLING INTO YOU

Words & Music by Rick Nowels, Marie-Claire D'Ubaldo & Billy Steinberg

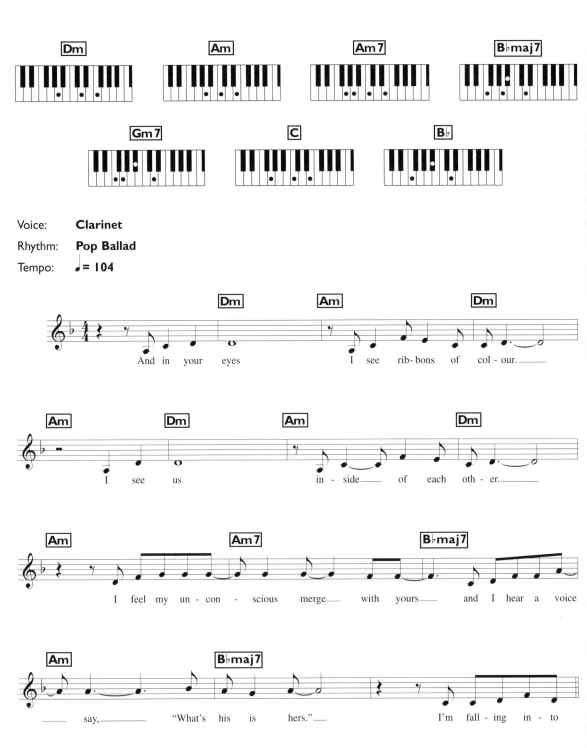

you. This dream could come true, and it feels

so good fall - ing in - to you. Fall - ing like a leaf,

fall - ing like a star,

find - ing a be - lief fall - ing where

you are. Fall -

- ing in - to you, fall - ing in - to you,

fall - ing in - to you.

FEMALE OF THE SPECIES

Words & Music by Tommy Scott, James Edwards, Francis Griffiths & Andrew Parle

FIELDS OF GOLD

Words & Music by Sting

FROM THIS MOMENT ON

Words & Music by Shania Twain & R. J. Lange

Voice: **Studio Piano**

Rhythm: **Pop Ballad**

Tempo: ♩ = 68

From this mo - ment___ life has be - gun,___ from this mo - ment___ you are the one,___ right be -

- side you   is where I   be - long,_____ from this   mo - ment   on.___ From this

mo - ment,___   I have been   blessed,__ I live on - ly   for your hap - pi - ness___ and for

your love,   I'd give my last   breath,_____ from this   mo - ment   on.___   I

GIMME GIMME GIMME (A MAN AFTER MIDNIGHT)

Words & Music by Benny Andersson & Björn Ulvaeus

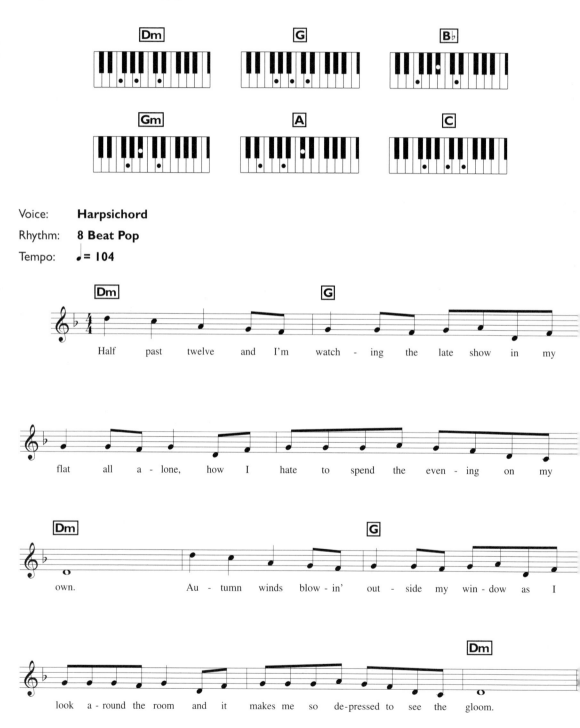

Voice: **Harpsichord**

Rhythm: **8 Beat Pop**

Tempo: ♩= 104

Half past twelve and I'm watch - ing the late show in my

flat all a - lone, how I hate to spend the even - ing on my

own. Au - tumn winds blow - in' out - side my win - dow as I

look a - round the room and it makes me so de - pressed to see the gloom.

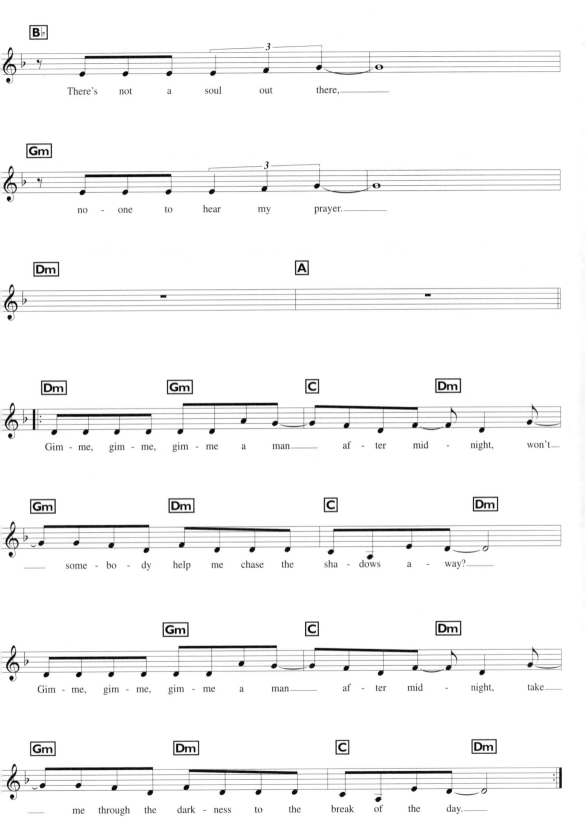

GOOD ENOUGH

Words & Music by Nigel Clark, Mathew Priest & Andy Miller

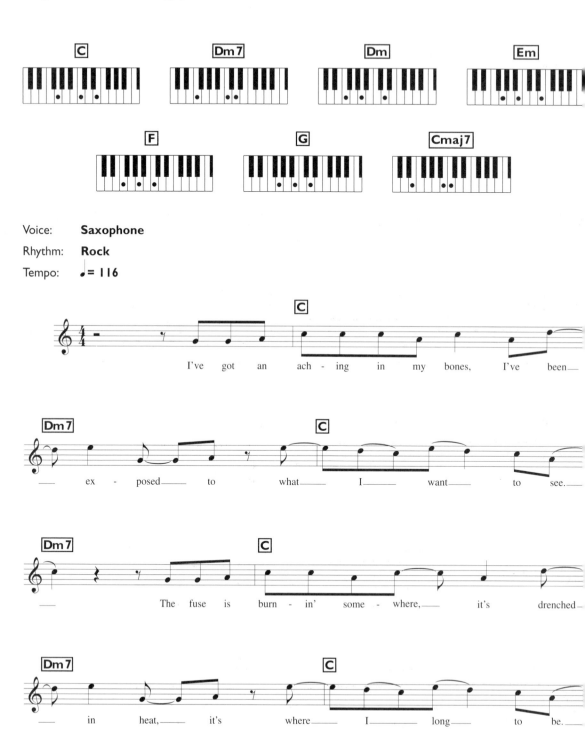

Voice: **Saxophone**

Rhythm: **Rock**

Tempo: ♩= 116

I've got an ach - ing in my bones, I've been

ex - posed to what I want to see.

The fuse is burn - in' some - where, it's drenched

in heat, it's where I long to be.

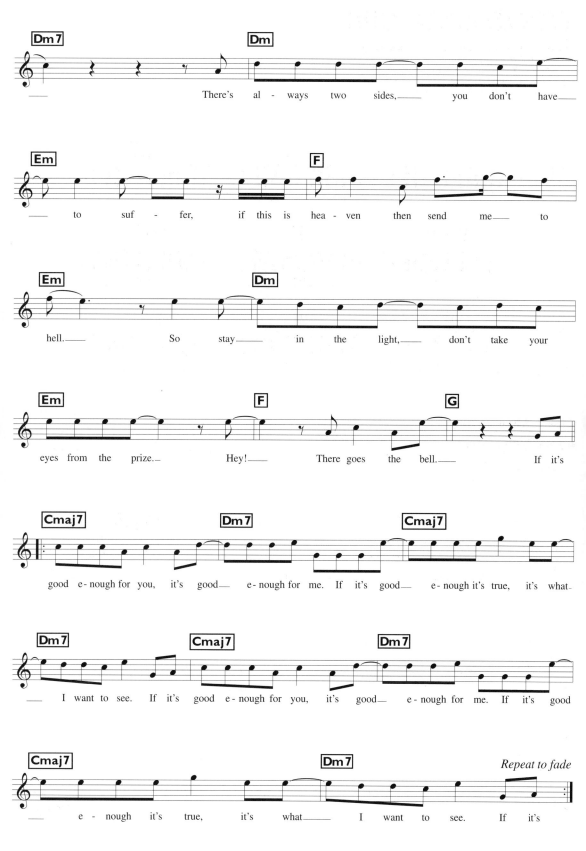

GOODNIGHT GIRL

Words & Music by Graeme Clark, Tom Cunningham,
Neil Mitchell & Marti Pellow

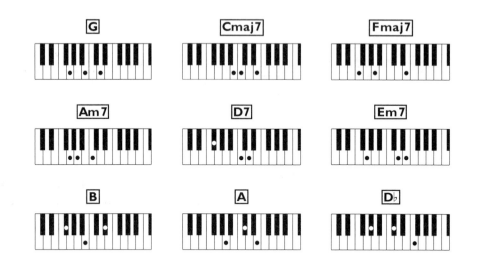

Voice: **Electric Guitar**

Rhythm: **Pop Rock**

Tempo: ♩= 112

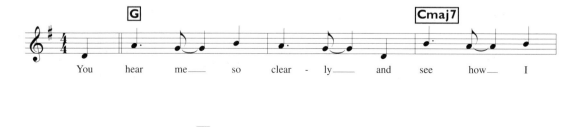

You hear me___ so clear - ly___ and see how___ I

try, you feel me,___ so heal me___ and

tear me___ a - part. And I won't tell a soul,___

GUAGLIONE

By Giovanni Fanciulli & Nisa
© Copyright 1956 (renewed 1984)
Accordo Edizioni Musicali, Milan, Italy.
Eaton Music Limited, 8 West Eaton Place, London SW1
for the UK, Eire, Australia & New Zealand.
All Rights Reserved. International Copyright Secured.

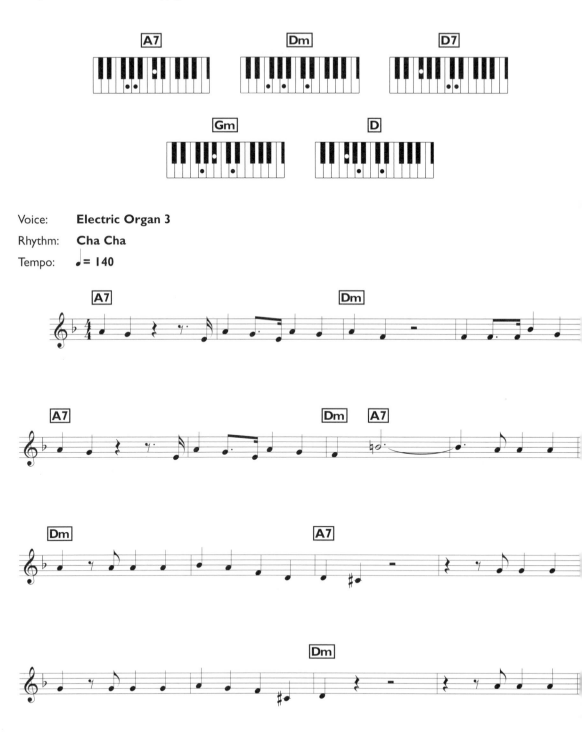

Voice: **Electric Organ 3**

Rhythm: **Cha Cha**

Tempo: ♩ = 140

HAVE I TOLD YOU LATELY

Words & Music by Van Morrison

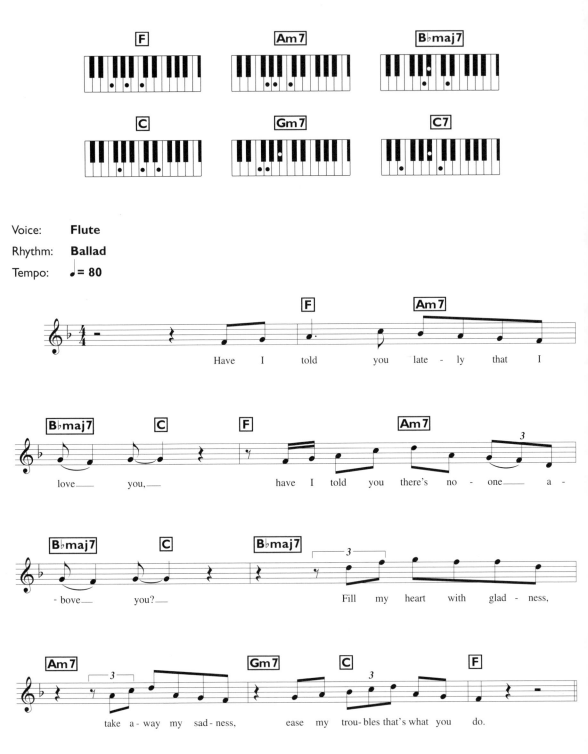

Voice: **Flute**

Rhythm: **Ballad**

Tempo: ♩= 80

HE AIN'T HEAVY... HE'S MY BROTHER

Words by Bob Russell
Music by Bobby Scott

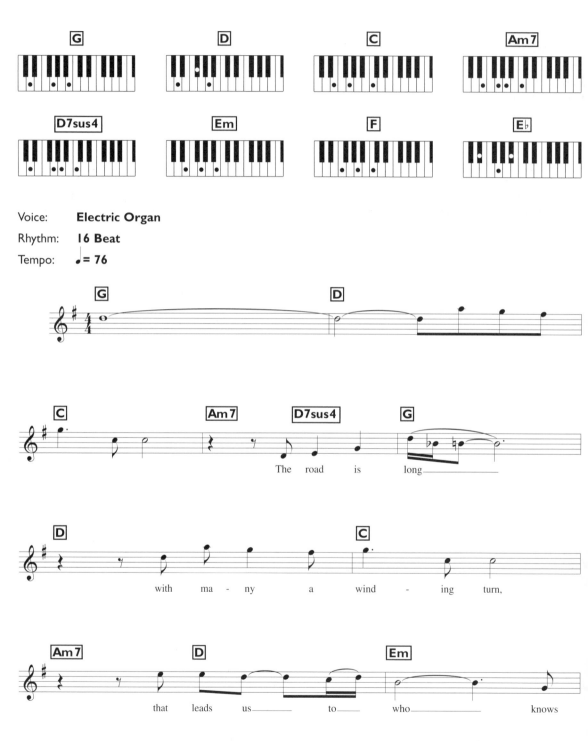

Voice: **Electric Organ**

Rhythm: **16 Beat**

Tempo: ♩ = 76

The road is long with ma-ny a wind - ing turn, that leads us to who knows

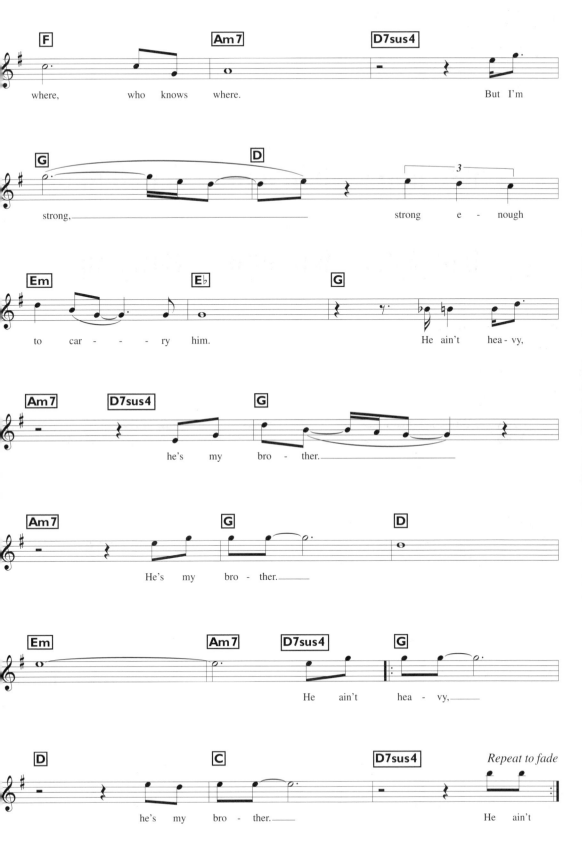

HIGH

Words by Paul Tucker
Music by Paul Tucker & Tunde Baiyewu
© Copyright 1997 Universal Music Publishing Limited,
77 Fulham Palace Road, London W6.
All Rights Reserved. International Copyright Secured.

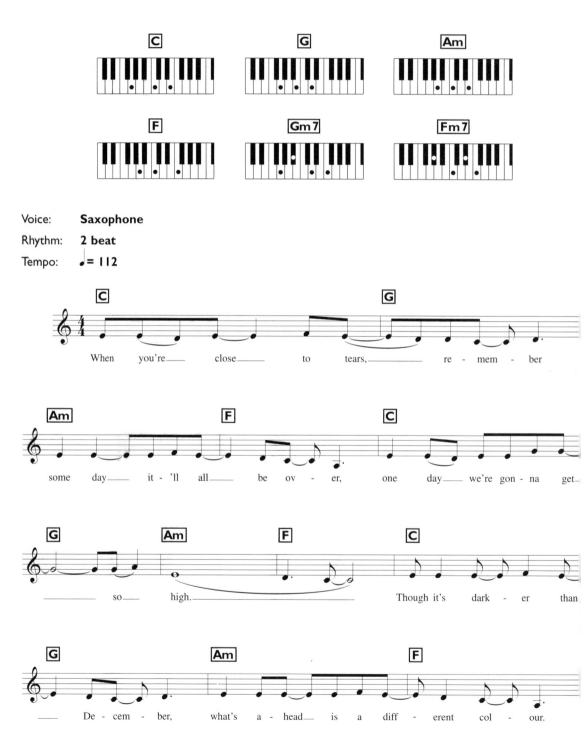

HOW DEEP IS YOUR LOVE

Words & Music by Barry Gibb, Robin Gibb & Maurice Gibb

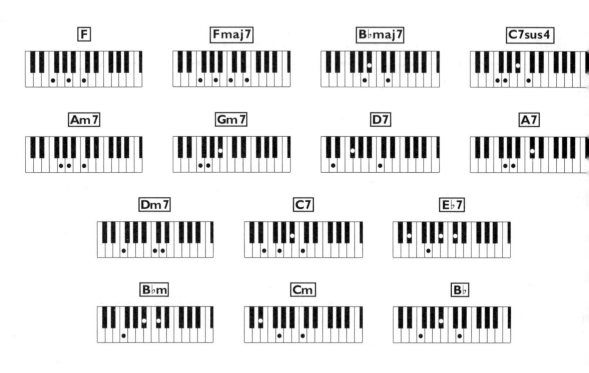

Voice: **Saxophone**

Rhythm: **Soft Rock**

Tempo: ♩ = 88

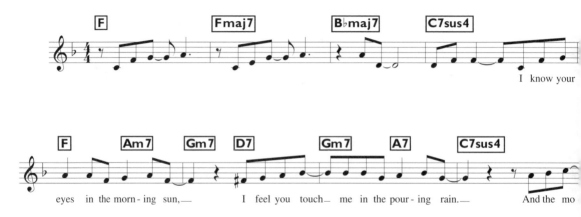

I know your

eyes in the morn-ing sun,— I feel you touch— me in the pour-ing rain.— And the mo

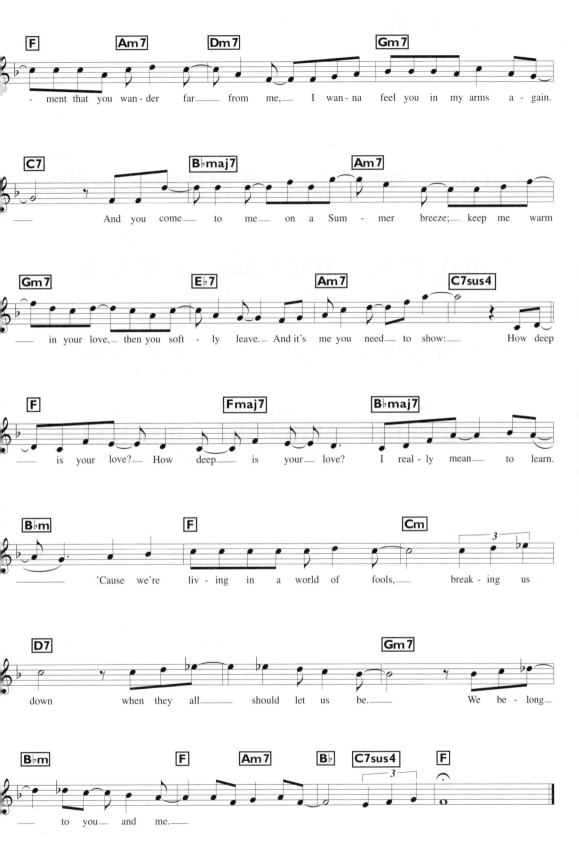

-ment that you wan-der far____ from me,____ I wan-na feel you in my arms a-gain.

And you come____ to me on a Sum - mer breeze;____ keep me warm

____ in your love,____ then you soft - ly leave.__ And it's me you need____ to show:____ How deep

____ is your love?__ How deep____ is your____ love? I real-ly mean____ to learn.

____ 'Cause we're liv-ing in a world of fools,____ break-ing us

down when they all____ should let us be.____ We be-long____

____ to you____ and me.____

I AM BLESSED

Words & Music by Marsha Malamet & Mark Mueller

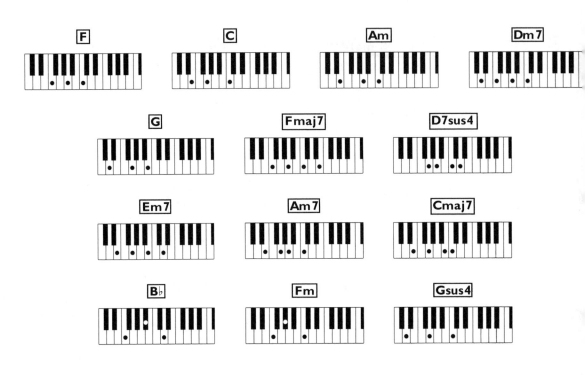

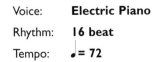

Voice: **Electric Piano**

Rhythm: **16 beat**

Tempo: ♩ = 72

Here in the si - lence I say a prayer, though I've nev-er seen you, some-how I know you're there. You're in the fa - ces of the

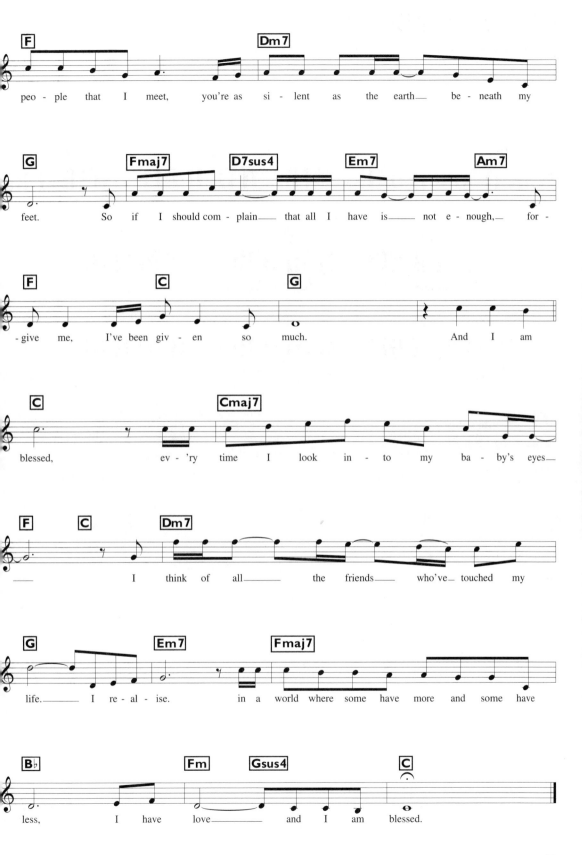

I BELIEVE I CAN FLY

Words & Music by Robert Kelly

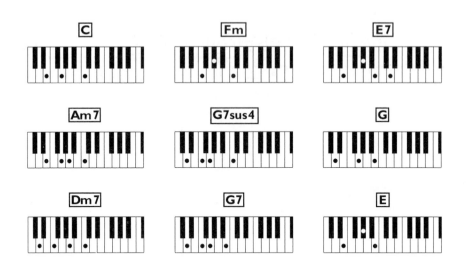

Voice: **Vibraphone**

Rhythm: **Soul Ballad**

Tempo: ♩ = 69

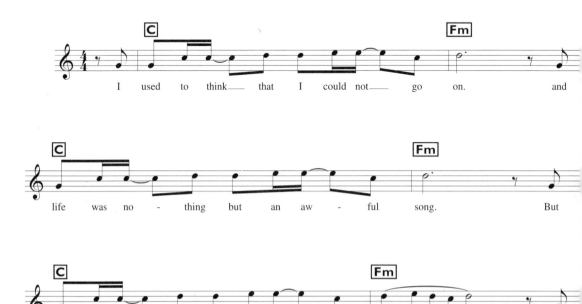

I used to think that I could not go on. and

life was no - thing but an aw - ful song. But

now I know the mean-ing of true love, I'm

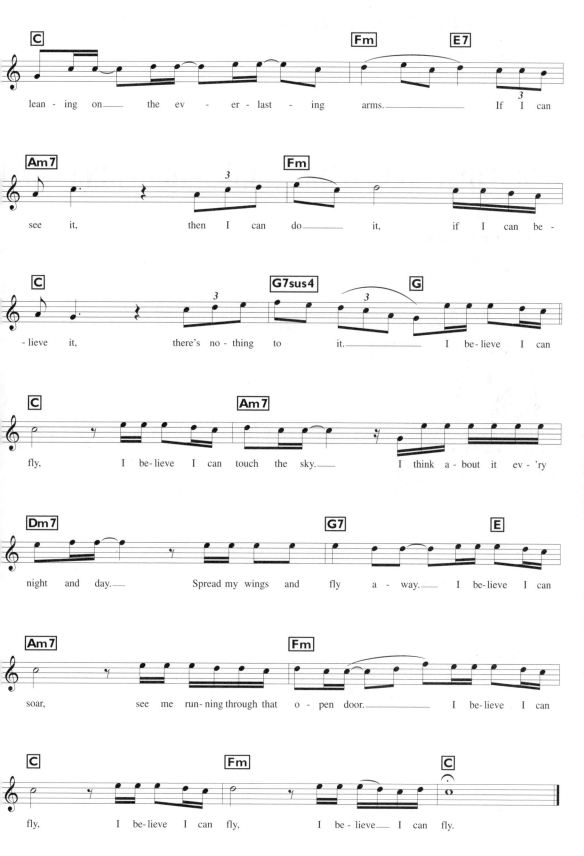

I JUST WANT TO MAKE LOVE TO YOU

Words & Music by Willie Dixon

keep you in-doors. There is no-thing for you to do_____ but

F7

keep me mak - ing love_____ to you. Love _____ to you,

C7

ooh_____ ooh,_____ love _____ to you. And I can

F7 **B♭** **F7** **B♭**

tell by the way you walk that walk, and I can hear by the way you

F7 **B♭** **F7**

talk that talk, and I can know by the way you treat your girl that I could

G7 **F7**

give you all the lov - in' in the whole wide world. Love _____ to you,

C7

Repeat to fade

ooh_____ ooh, _____ love_____ to you.

I WILL ALWAYS LOVE YOU

Words & Music by Dolly Parton
© Copyright 1975 Velvet Apple Music, USA.
Carlin Music Corporation, Iron Bridge House, 3 Bridge Approach, London NW1.
All Rights Reserved. International Copyright Secured.

Voice: **Ocarina**

Rhythm: **Ballad**

Tempo: ♩ **= 76**

I WILL SURVIVE

Words & Music by Dino Fekaris & Freddie Perren

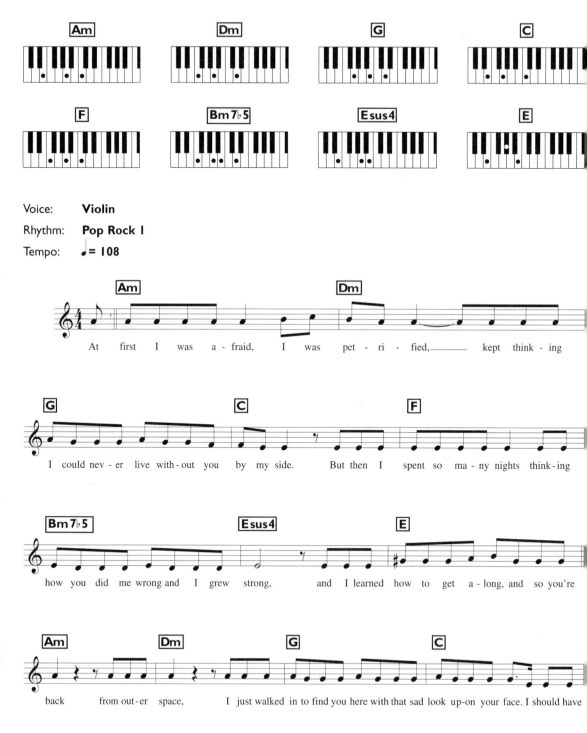

I'M YOUR ANGEL

Words & Music by R. Kelly

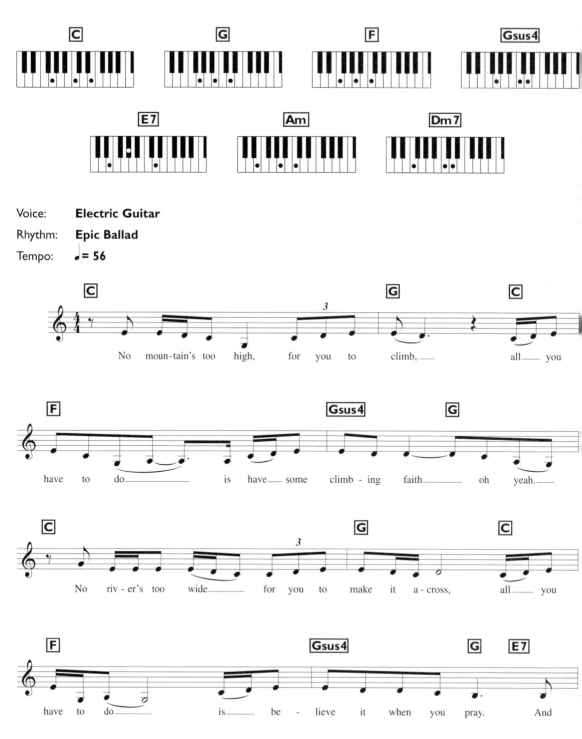

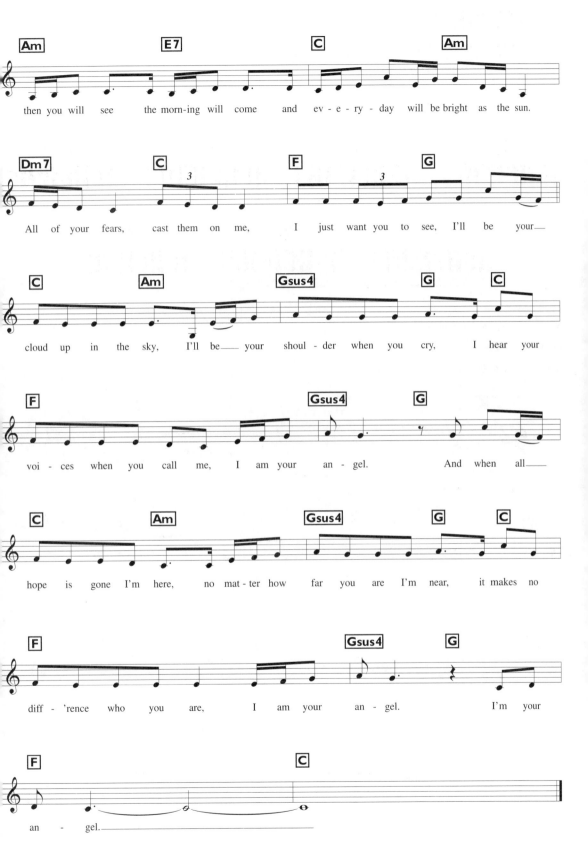

then you will see the morn-ing will come and ev-e-ry-day will be bright as the sun.

All of your fears, cast them on me, I just want you to see, I'll be your

cloud up in the sky, I'll be your shoul-der when you cry, I hear your

voi-ces when you call me, I am your an-gel. And when all

hope is gone I'm here, no mat-ter how far you are I'm near, it makes no

diff-'rence who you are, I am your an-gel. I'm your

an-gel.

IMAGINE

Words & Music by John Lennon

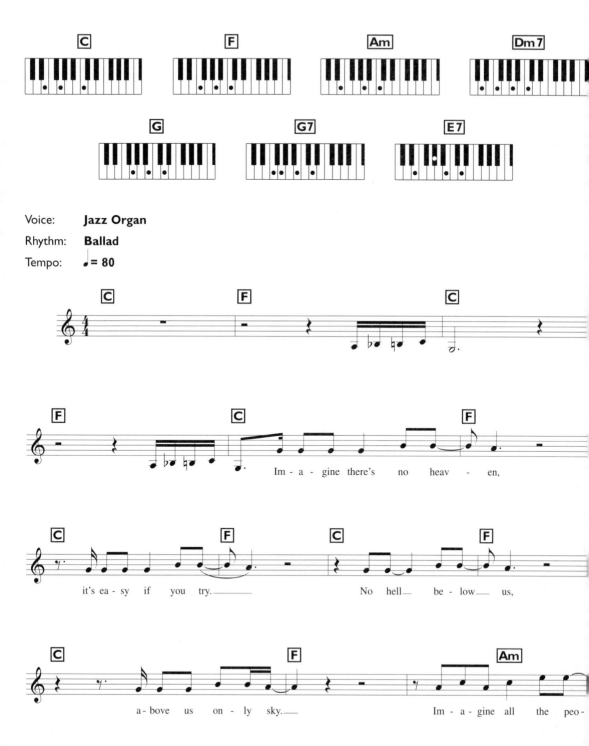

Voice: **Jazz Organ**

Rhythm: **Ballad**

Tempo: ♩ = 80

Im - a - gine there's no heav - en,

it's ea - sy if you try._____ No hell___ be - low___ us,

a - bove us on - ly sky.___ Im - a - gine all the peo-

IRONIC

Words by Alanis Morissette
Music by Alanis Morissette & Glenn Ballard

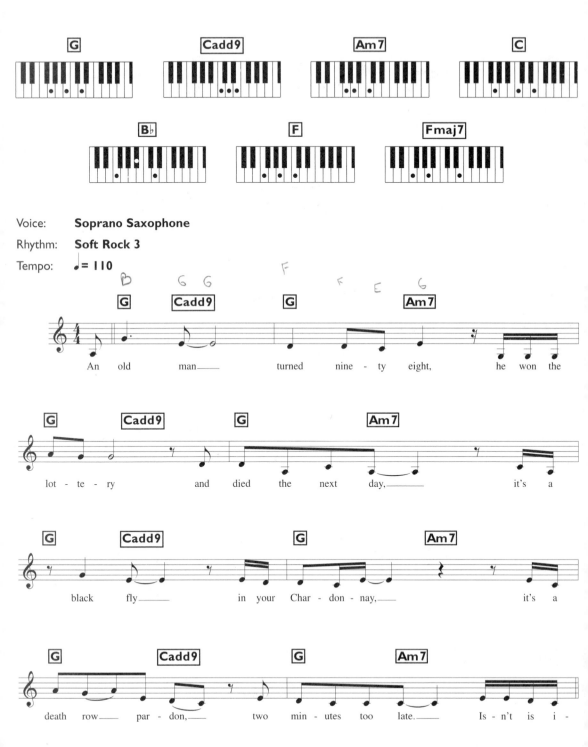

- ron - ic,   don't you think?   It's like rain_____   on your

wed - ding   day.____   It's a free____   ride,_____   when you're al - rea - dy   paid,____   it's the good ad -

- vice,   that you just did - n't take,____   who would - 've   thought____   it   fig -

- ures._____   And____   you   know

life   has   a   fun - ny   way   of   sneak - ing   up   on   you._____

Life   has   a   fun - ny,   fun - ny   way____   of   help - ing   you   out,____

____   help - ing   you   out.

IT'S ALL COMING BACK TO ME NOW

Words & Music by Jim Steinman

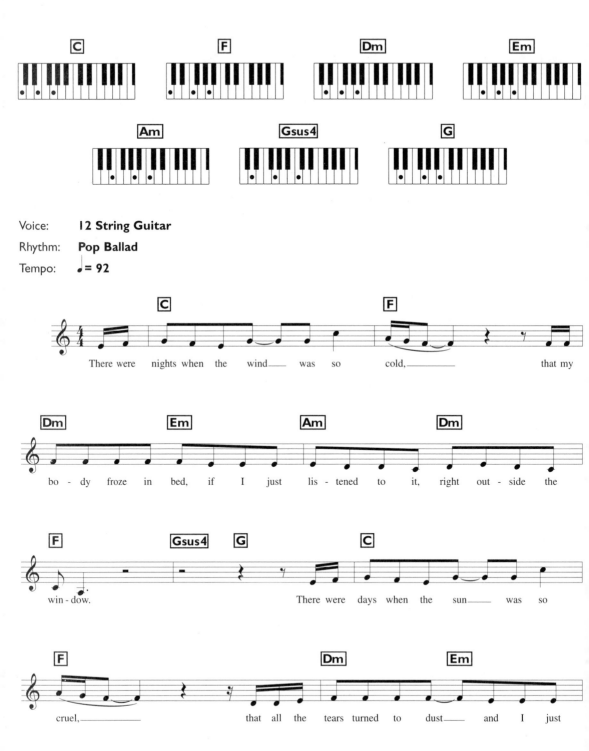

Voice: **12 String Guitar**

Rhythm: **Pop Ballad**

Tempo: ♩ = 92

There were nights when the wind___ was so cold, ___ that my bo - dy froze in bed, if I just lis - tened to it, right out - side the win - dow. There were days when the sun___ was so cruel, ___ that all the tears turned to dust___ and I just

KILLING ME SOFTLY WITH HIS SONG

Words by Norman Gimbel
Music by Charles Fox

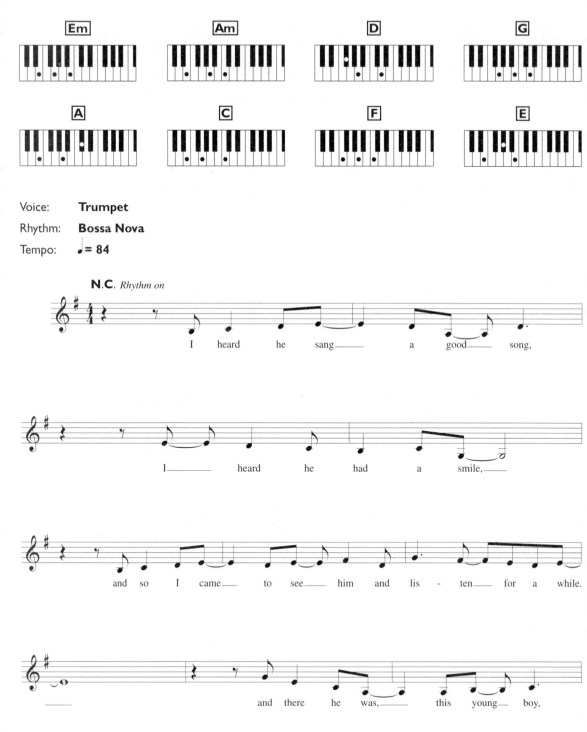

Voice: **Trumpet**

Rhythm: **Bossa Nova**

Tempo: ♩ = 84

KNOWING ME, KNOWING YOU

Words & Music by Benny Andersson, Björn Ulvaeus & Stig Anderson

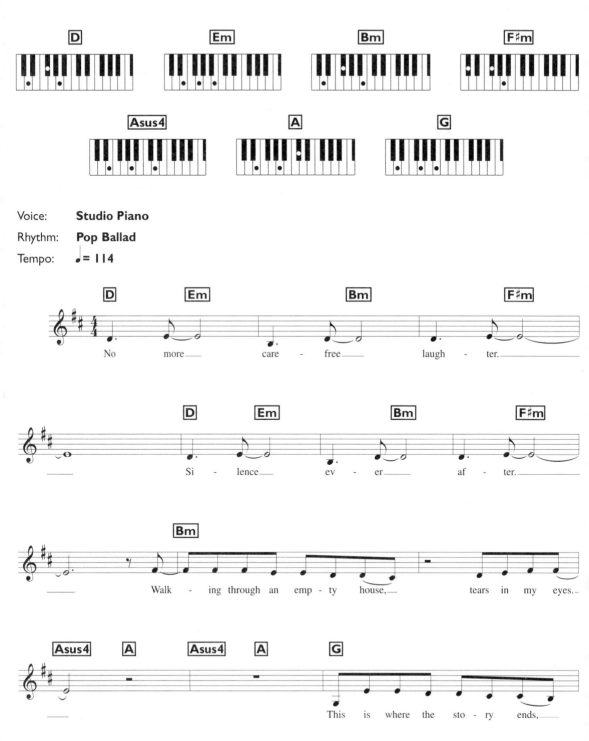

LAST THING ON MY MIND

Words by Sarah Dallin & Keren Woodward
Music by Mike Stock & Pete Waterman

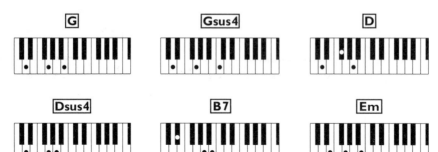

Voice: **Studio Piano**
Rhythm: **Lite Pop**
Tempo: ♩= 124

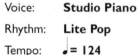

There was some - thing in your voice that was tell -

- ing me don't be too sure, a - rous-ing my sus - pi - cions, I have ne -

- ver felt be - fore. I thought we had it made,

LIFTED

Words & Music by Paul Tucker, Emmanuel Baiyewu & Martin Brammer
© *Copyright 1994 Lots Of Hits Music Limited.*
Universal Music Publishing Limited, 77 Fulham Palace Road, London W6.
All Rights Reserved. International Copyright Secured.

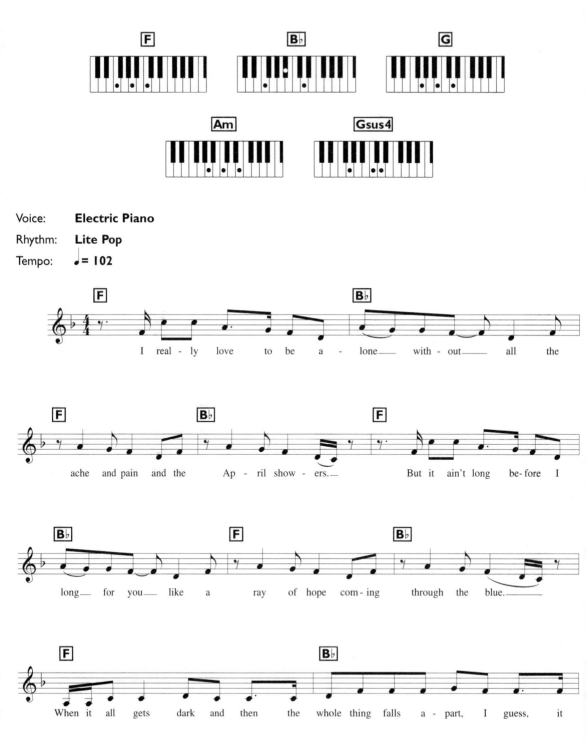

Voice: **Electric Piano**

Rhythm: **Lite Pop**

Tempo: ♩ = 102

I real-ly love to be a - lone— with - out— all the

ache and pain and the Ap - ril show - ers.— But it ain't long be-fore I

long— for you— like a ray of hope com-ing through the blue.—

When it all gets dark and then the whole thing falls a - part, I guess, it

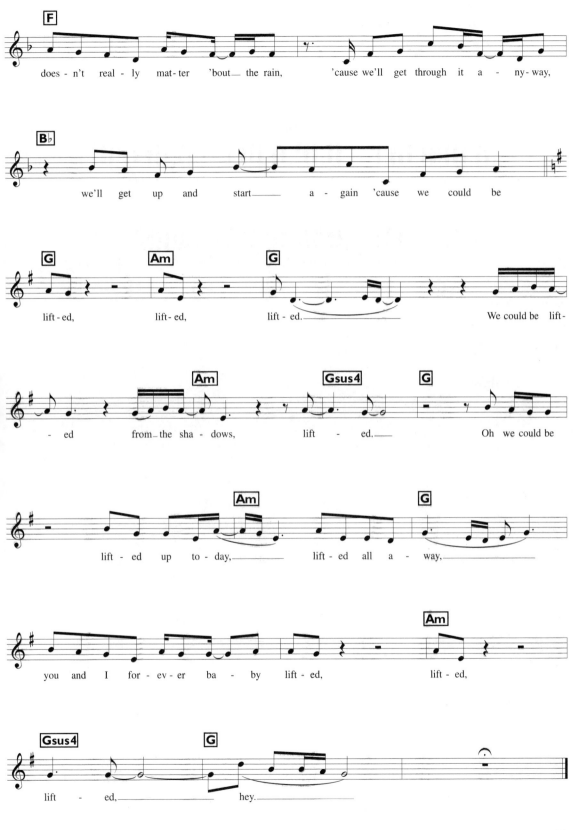

LIVIN' LA VIDA LOCA

Words & Music by Desmond Child & Robi Rosa

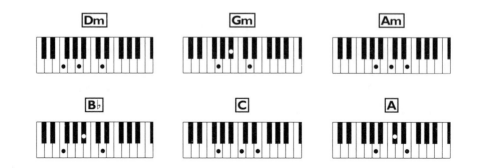

Voice: **Piano 2**

Rhythm: **Samba**

Tempo: ♩ = 88

She's in-to su-per-sti-tion, black cats and voo-doo dolls ___

and I feel a pre-mo-ni-tion, that girl's gon-na make me fall. ___

She's in-to new sen-sa-tions, new kicks in the can-dle-light. ___

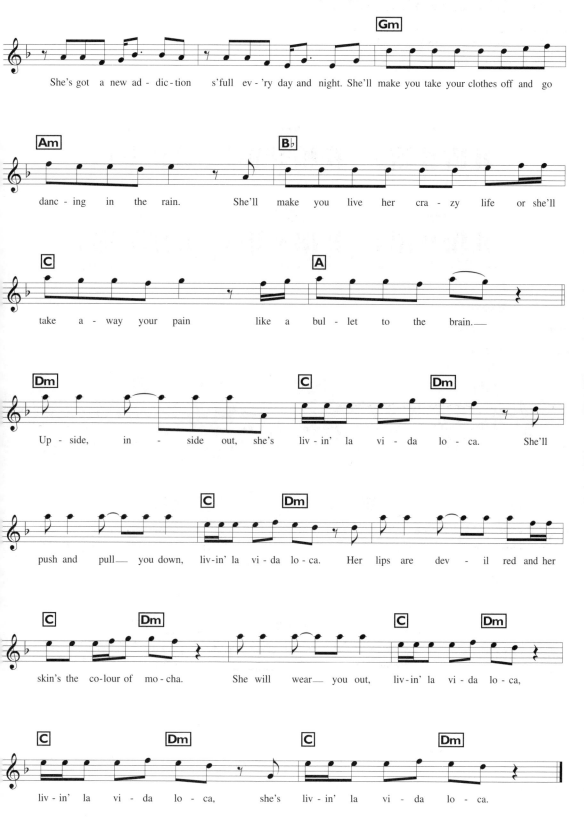

THE LOCO-MOTION

Words & Music by Gerry Goffin & Carole King

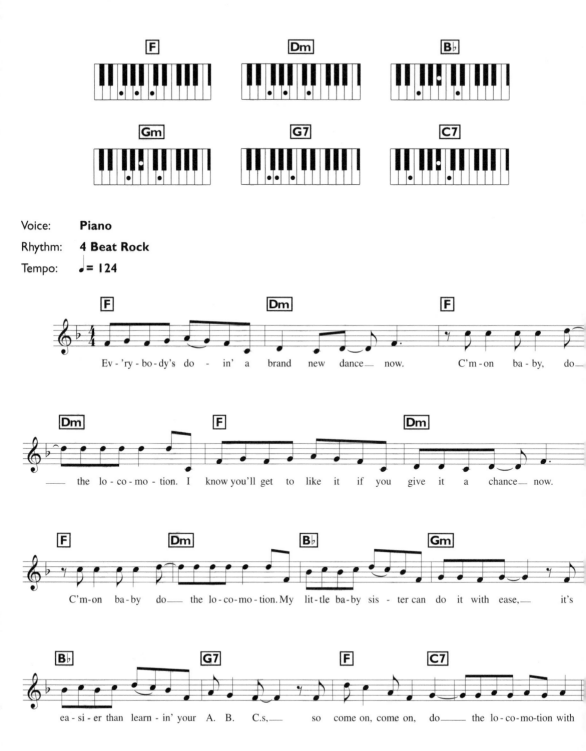

Voice: **Piano**

Rhythm: **4 Beat Rock**

Tempo: ♩ = 124

Ev - 'ry - bo - dy's do - in' a brand new dance— now. C'm - on ba - by, do—

— the lo - co - mo - tion. I know you'll get to like it if you give it a chance— now.

C'm - on ba - by do— the lo - co - mo - tion. My lit - tle ba - by sis - ter can do it with ease, it's

ea - si - er than learn - in' your A. B. C.s,— so come on, come on, do— the lo - co - mo - tion with

LOVE IS ALL AROUND

Words & Music by Reg Presley
© Copyright 1967 Dick James Music Limited.
Universal/Dick James Music Limited, 77 Fulham Palace Road, London W6.
All Rights Reserved. International Copyright Secured.

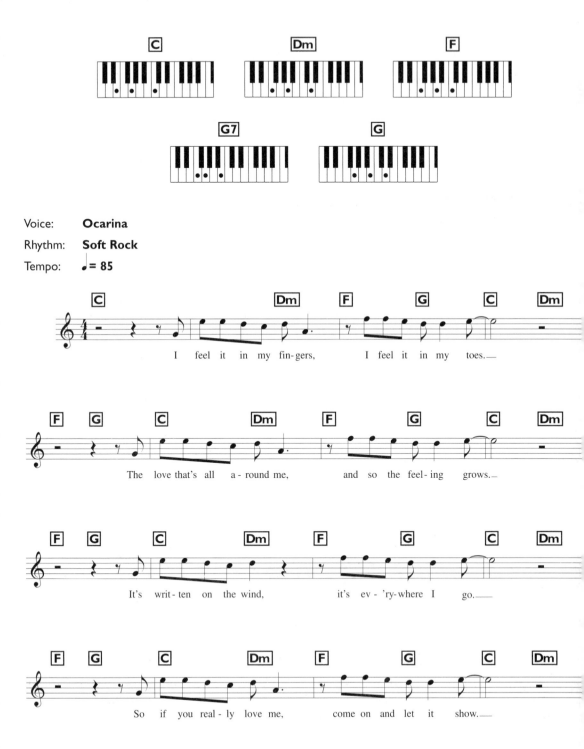

Voice: **Ocarina**

Rhythm: **Soft Rock**

Tempo: ♩ = 85

I feel it in my fin-gers, I feel it in my toes.—

The love that's all a-round me, and so the feel-ing grows.—

It's writ-ten on the wind, it's ev-'ry-where I go.—

So if you real-ly love me, come on and let it show.—

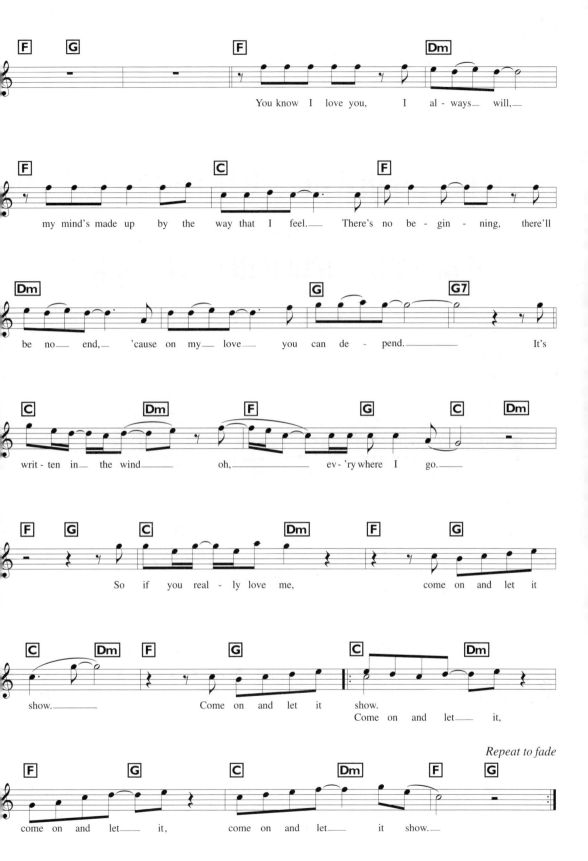

You know I love you, I al - ways_ will,_ my mind's made up by the way that I feel._ There's no be - gin - ning, there'll be no_ end,_ 'cause on my_ love_ you can de - pend._ It's writ - ten in_ the wind_ oh,_ ev - 'ry where I go._ So if you real - ly love me, come on and let it show._ Come on and let it show. Come on and let_ it, come on and let_ it, come on and let_ it show._

Repeat to fade

MAMMA MIA

Words & Music by Benny Andersson, Björn Ulvaeus & Stig Anderson

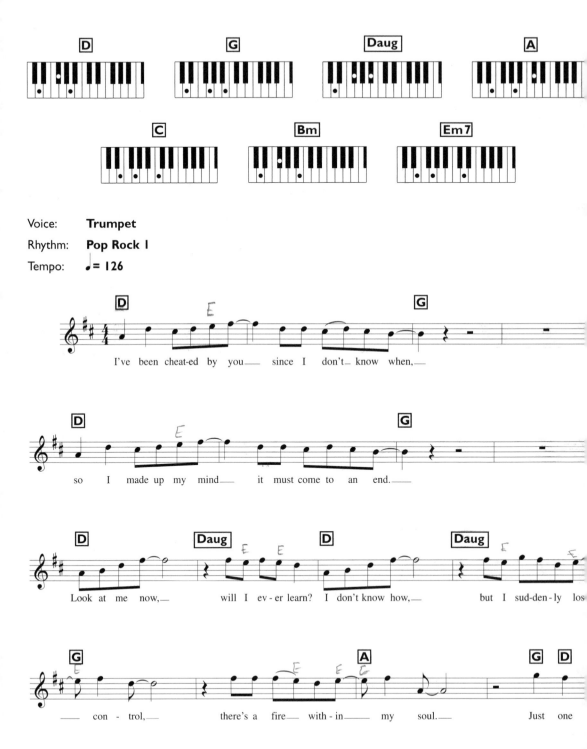

Voice: **Trumpet**

Rhythm: **Pop Rock 1**

Tempo: ♩= 126

I've been cheat-ed by you since I don't know when,

so I made up my mind it must come to an end.

Look at me now, will I ev-er learn? I don't know how, but I sud-den-ly los

con-trol, there's a fire with-in my soul. Just one

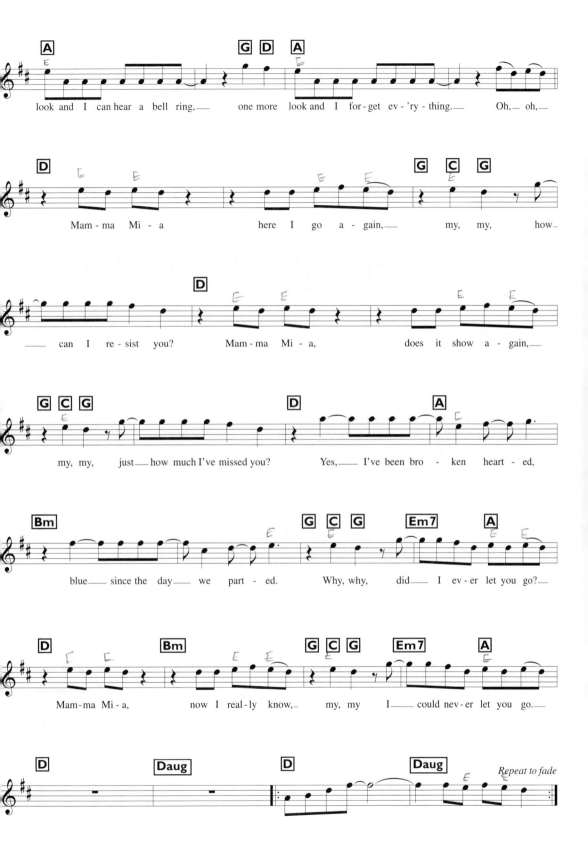

MAN! I FEEL LIKE A WOMAN!

Words & Music by Shania Twain & R.J. Lange

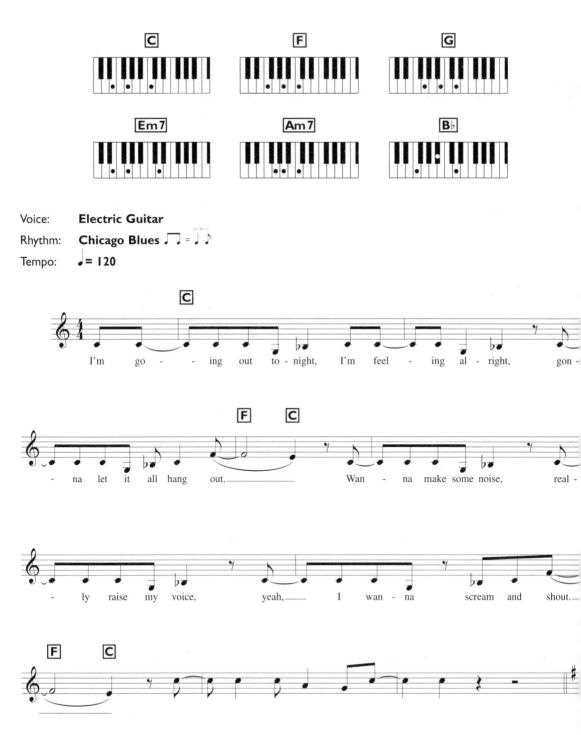

Oh— oh oh,— go to-tal-ly cra-zy,— for-get I'm a la-dy,—

men's shirts, short skirts. Oh— oh oh,— real-ly go wild, yeah,—

do-ing it in style.— Oh— oh oh,— get in the ac-tion,—

feel the at-trac-tion,— co-lour my hair, what do I dare?

Oh— oh oh,— I wan-na be free, yeah, to

feel the way I feel.—

I feel like a wo-man.

MARVELLOUS

Words & Music by Ian Broudie
© *Copyright 1994 Chrysalis Music Limited, The Chrysalis Building,*
Bramley Road, London W10.
All Rights Reserved. International Copyright Secured.

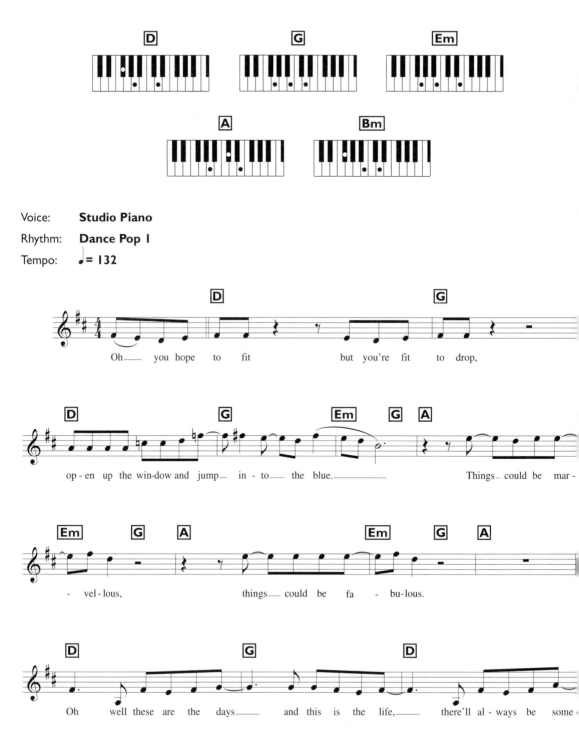

Voice:	**Studio Piano**
Rhythm:	**Dance Pop 1**
Tempo:	♩= 132

MI CHICO LATINO

Words & Music by Geri Halliwell, Andy Watkins & Paul Wilson

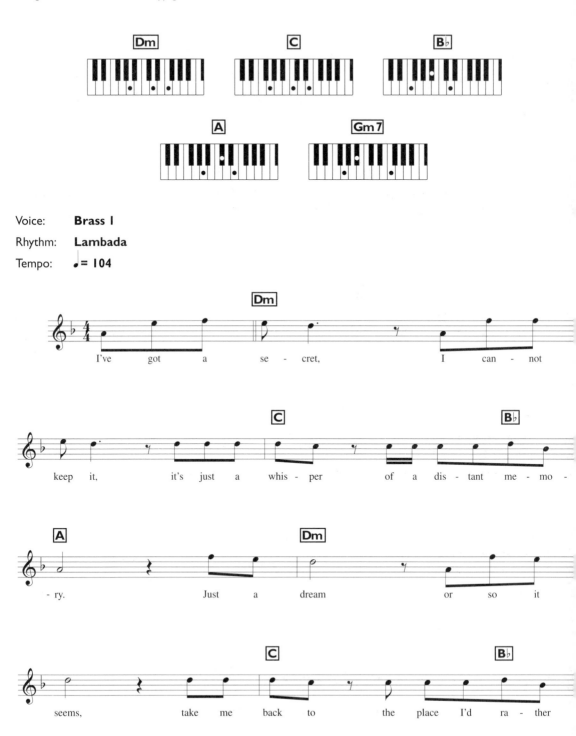

Voice: **Brass 1**

Rhythm: **Lambada**

Tempo: ♩ = 104

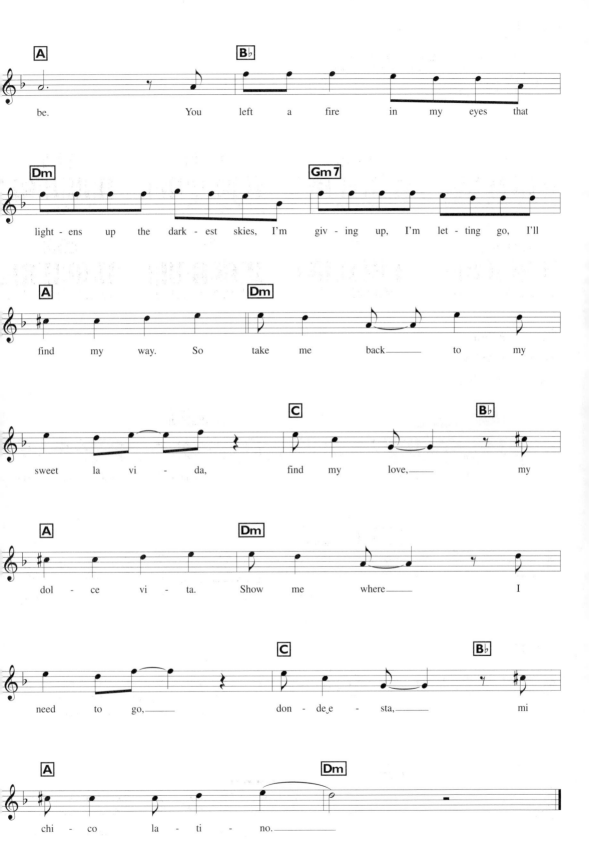

be. You left a fire in my eyes that

light - ens up the dark - est skies, I'm giv - ing up, I'm let - ting go, I'll

find my way. So take me back to my

sweet la vi - da, find my love, my

dol - ce vi - ta. Show me where I

need to go, don - de e - sta, mi

chi - co la - ti - no.

MISSING

Words & Music by Tracey Thorn & Ben Watt

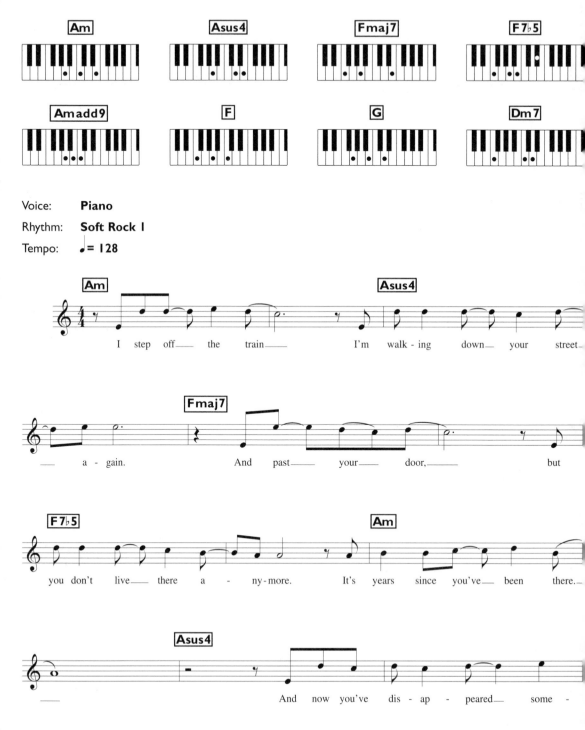

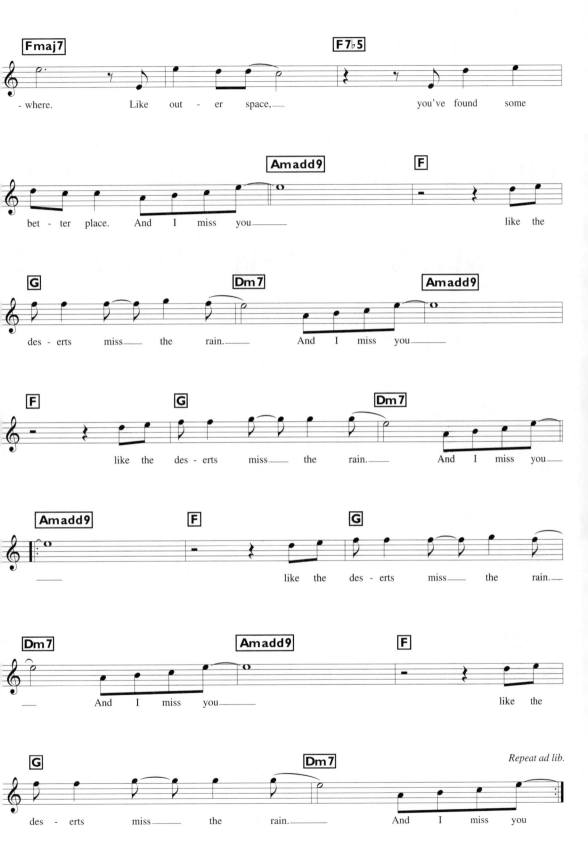

MORE THAN A WOMAN

Words & Music by Barry Gibb, Robin Gibb & Maurice Gibb
© Copyright 1977 Gibb Brothers Music.
All Rights Reserved. International Copyright Secured.

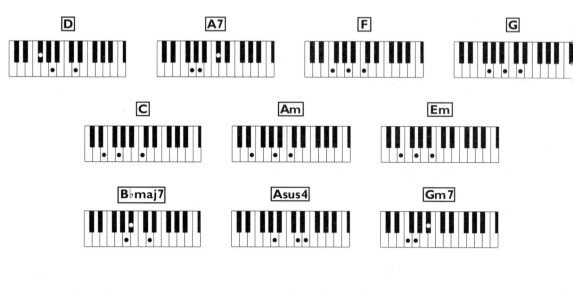

Voice: **Distortion Guitar**

Rhythm: **Techno**

Tempo: ♩ = 110

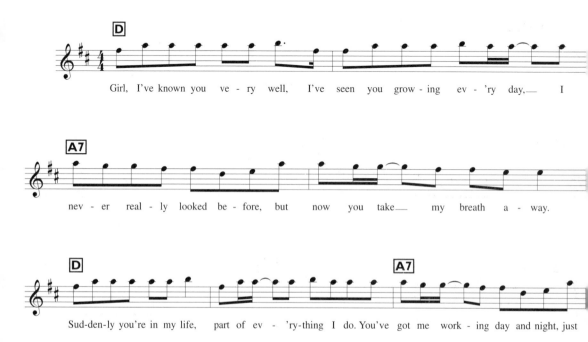

Girl, I've known you ve - ry well, I've seen you grow - ing ev - 'ry day,— I

nev - er real - ly looked be - fore, but now you take— my breath a - way.

Sud-den-ly you're in my life, part of ev - 'ry-thing I do. You've got me work - ing day and night, just

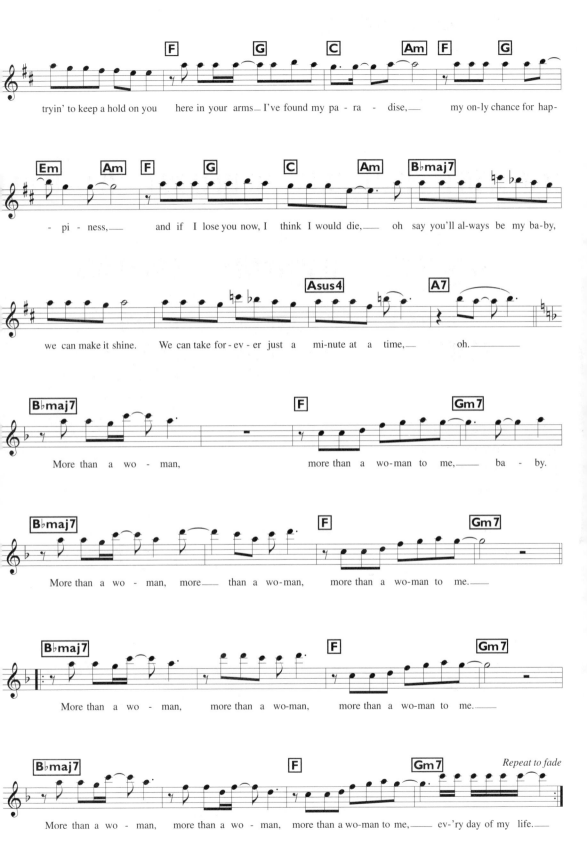

tryin' to keep a hold on you   here in your arms— I've found my pa - ra - dise,— my on-ly chance for hap-

- pi - ness,— and if I lose you now, I think I would die,— oh say you'll al-ways be my ba-by,

we can make it shine.   We can take for-ev-er just a mi-nute at a time,— oh.—

More than a wo - man,   more than a wo-man to me,— ba - by.

More than a wo - man, more— than a wo-man, more than a wo-man to me.—

More than a wo - man, more than a wo-man, more than a wo-man to me.—

More than a wo - man, more than a wo-man, more than a wo-man to me,— ev-'ry day of my life.—

MORE THAN WORDS

Words & Music by Nuno Bettencourt & Gary Cherone

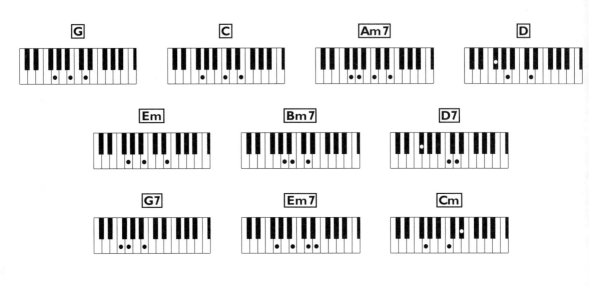

Voice: **Saxophone**

Rhythm: **Soft Rock**

Tempo: ♩ = 88

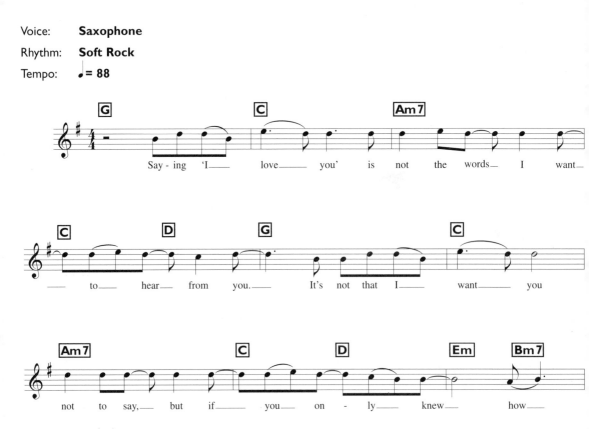

Say-ing 'I love you' is not the words I want to hear from you. It's not that I want you not to say, but if you on-ly knew how

ea - sy____ it would be____ to____ show____ me how____ you feel,____

____ more than words_____ is all you have____ to____ do

____ to make____ it____ real.____ Then you would - n't have____ to say____

____ that you love____ me,____ 'cause I'd____ al - rea - dy____

know. What would you say____ if I took____

____ those words____ a - way,____ then you could - n't make____ things new____

____ just by say - ing 'I____ love____ you'.

NEVER EVER

Words & Music by Shaznay Lewis, Esmail Jazayeri & Sean Mather
© Copyright 1997 Rickidy Raw Music/BMG Music Publishing Limited,
Bedford House, 69-79 Fulham High Street, London SW6 (40%) &
Universal/MCA Music Limited, 77 Fulham Palace Road, London W6 (60%).
This arrangement © Copyright 2000 BMG Music Publishing Limited for their share of interest.
All Rights Reserved. International Copyright Secured.

Voice: **Saxophone**

Rhythm: **16 beat**

Tempo: ♩ = **72**

My head's spin - ning,___ boy I'm in___ a daze,___ I feel i - so - lat - ed,___

don't wan-na com-mu - ni - cate.___ I'll take a show-er, I will___ scour,___ I will run___

___ find peace of mind,_ the hap-py mind, I once___ owned___ yeah. Flex-in' vo-cab-u-la-ry runs right through me.

The al-pha-bet runs right from A to Z. Con-ver - sa-tions, he - si - ta-tions in___ my mind,

you got my con-science ask-ing ques-tions that I can't find. I'm not cra - zy.___ I'm

sure I ain't done no-thing wrong. No, I'm just wait - ing,— 'cause I heard that this feeling won't last— that long.—

Nev-er ev-er have I ev-er felt so low, when you gon-na take me out of this black hole?

Nev-er ev-er have I ev-er felt so sad. The way I'm feel-ing, yeah you got me feel-ing real - ly bad.

Nev-er ev-er have I had to find, I've had to dig a - way to find my own peace of mind.

I nev-er ev-er had my con-science to fight, the way I'm feel-ing yeah it just don't feel right.

Nev-er ev-er have I ev-er felt so low, when you gon-na take me out of this black hole?

Nev-er ev-er have I ev-er felt so sad. The way I'm feel-ing, yeah you got me feel-ing real - ly bad.

Nev-er ev-er have I had to find, I've had to dig a - way to find my own peace of mind.

I nev-er ev-er had my conscience to fight, the way I'm feel-ing yeah it just don't feel right.—

NO MATTER WHAT

Music by Andrew Lloyd Webber
Lyrics by Jim Steinman

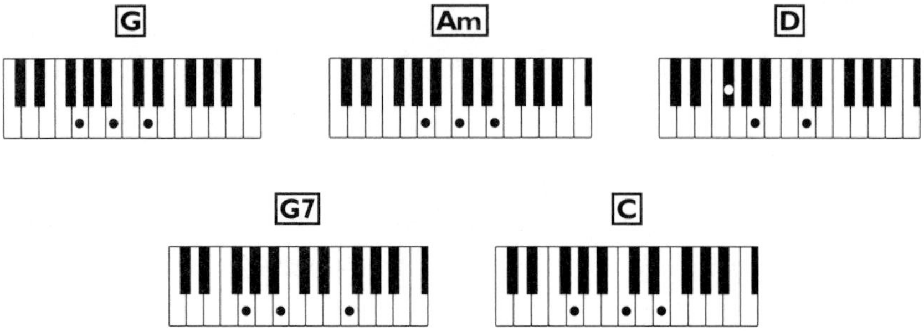

Voice: **Choir**

Rhythm: **Light Pop**

Tempo: ♩ = 106

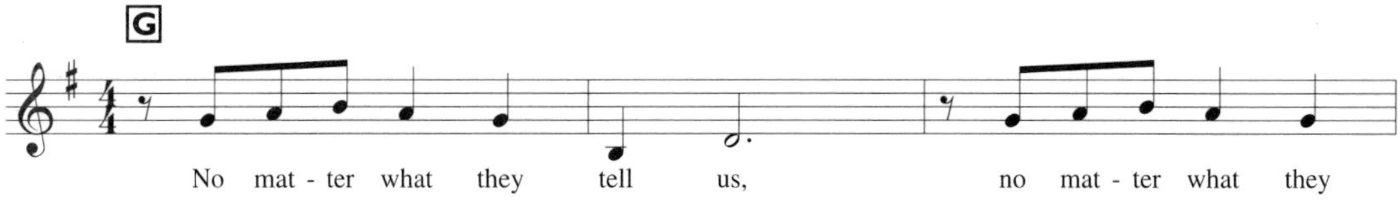

No mat-ter what they tell us, no mat-ter what they do.

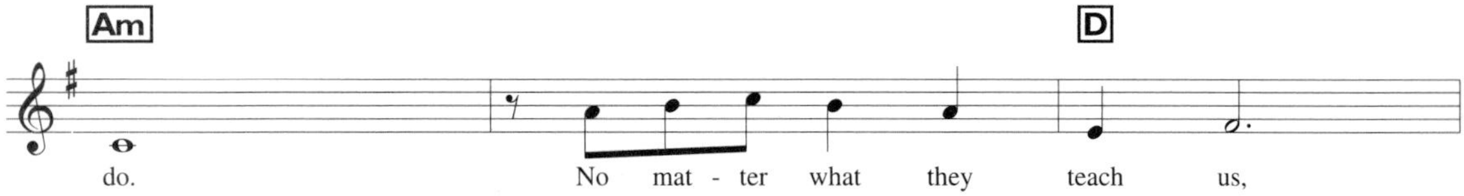

No mat-ter what they teach us, what we be-lieve is true.

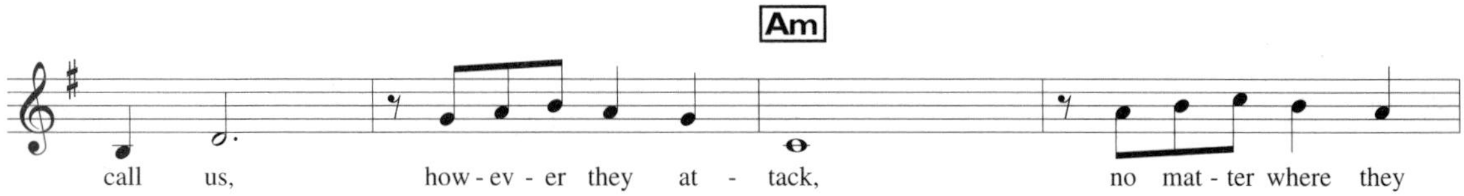

No mat-ter what they call us, how-ev-er they at-tack, no mat-ter where they

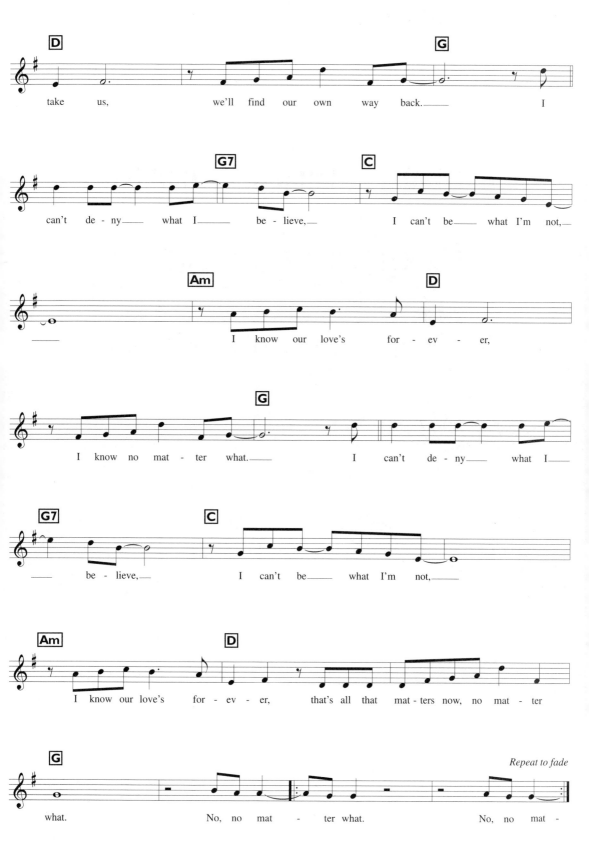

take us,   we'll find   our   own   way   back._____   I

can't   de - ny____   what I____   be - lieve,____   I   can't   be____   what I'm   not,____

____   I   know   our   love's   for - ev - er,

I   know   no   mat - ter   what.____   I   can't   de - ny____   what   I____

be - lieve,____   I   can't   be____   what   I'm   not,____

I   know   our   love's   for - ev - er,   that's   all   that   mat - ters   now,   no   mat - ter

Repeat to fade

what.   No,   no   mat - ter   what.   No,   no   mat -

PERFECT MOMENT

Words & Music by James Marr & Wendy Page

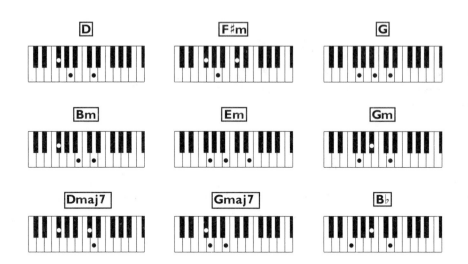

Voice: **Electric Guitar 2**

Rhythm: **Pop Ballad**

Tempo: ♩ = 68

This is my mo-ment, this is my per-fect mo-ment with you.

This is what God meant this is my per-fect mo-ment with

you. Wish I could freeze this space in

PICTURE OF YOU

Words & Music by Eliot Kennedy, Ronan Keating, Paul Wilson & Andy Watkins
© Copyright 1997 Universal/Island Music Limited, 77 Fulham Palace Road, London W6 (10%),
Sony/ATV Music Publishing (UK) Limited, 10 Great Marlborough Street, London W1 (25%) &
19 Music Limited/BMG Music Publishing Limited, Bedford House, 69-79 Fulham High Street, London SW6 (65%).
This arrangement © Copyright 2000 BMG Music Publishing Limited for their share of interest.
All Rights Reserved. International Copyright Secured.

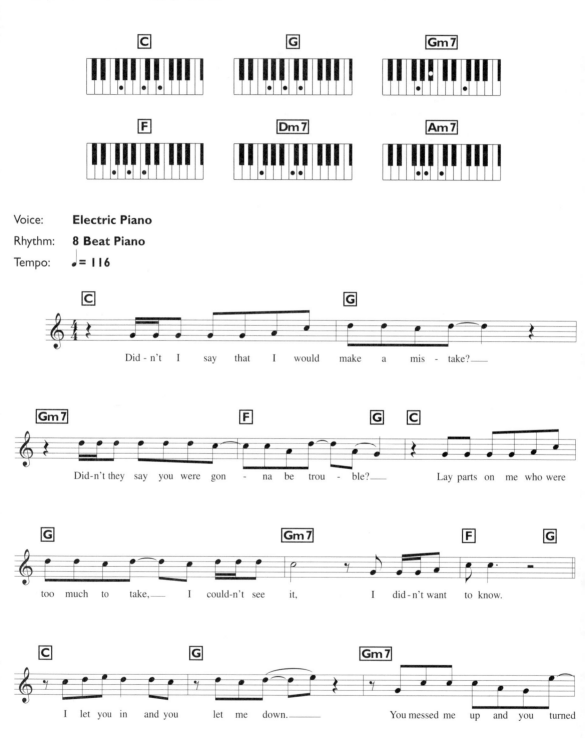

Voice: **Electric Piano**

Rhythm: **8 Beat Piano**

Tempo: ♩ = 116

Did-n't I say that I would make a mis-take?

Did-n't they say you were gon - na be trou-ble? Lay parts on me who were

too much to take, I could-n't see it, I did-n't want to know.

I let you in and you let me down. You messed me up and you turned

Repeat to fade

THE POWER OF LOVE

Words & Music by Candy de Rouge, Gunther Mende, Jennifer Rush & Susan Applegate
© Copyright 1985 EMI Songs Musikverlag GmbH.
EMI Songs Limited, 127 Charing Cross Road, London WC2.
All Rights Reserved. International Copyright Secured.

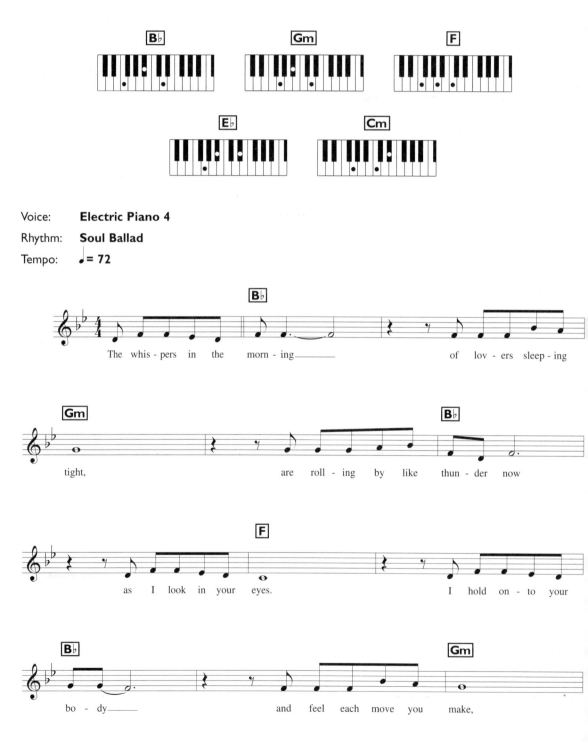

Voice: **Electric Piano 4**

Rhythm: **Soul Ballad**

Tempo: ♩ = 72

The whis - pers in the morn - ing_____ of lov - ers sleep - ing

tight, are roll - ing by like thun - der now

as I look in your eyes. I hold on - to your

bo - dy_____ and feel each move you make,

ROAD RAGE

Words & Music by Cerys Matthews, Mark Roberts,
Aled Richards, Paul Jones & Owen Powell
© Copyright 1997 Sony/ATV Music Publishing (UK) Limited,
10 Great Marlborough Street, London W1.
All Rights Reserved. International Copyright Secured.

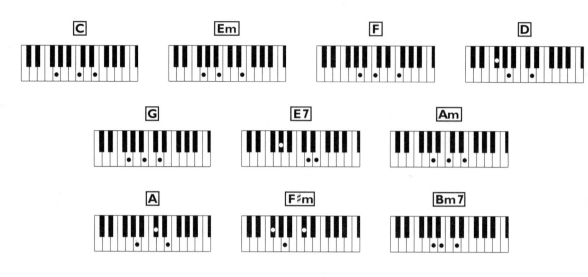

Voice: **Distortion Guitar**

Rhythm: **Soft Rock 1**

Tempo: ♩ = 96

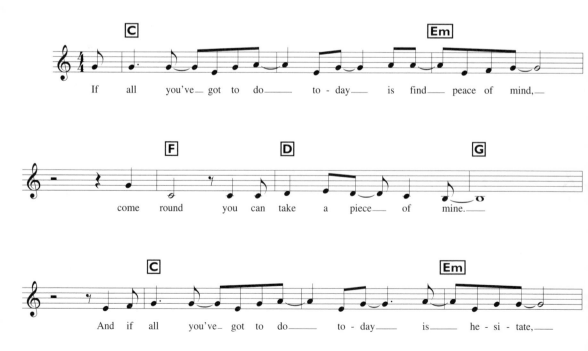

ROTTERDAM

Words & Music by Paul Heaton & David Rotheray
© Copyright 1996 Island Music Limited.
Universal/Island Music Limited, 77 Fulham Palace Road, London W6.
All Rights Reserved. International Copyright Secured.

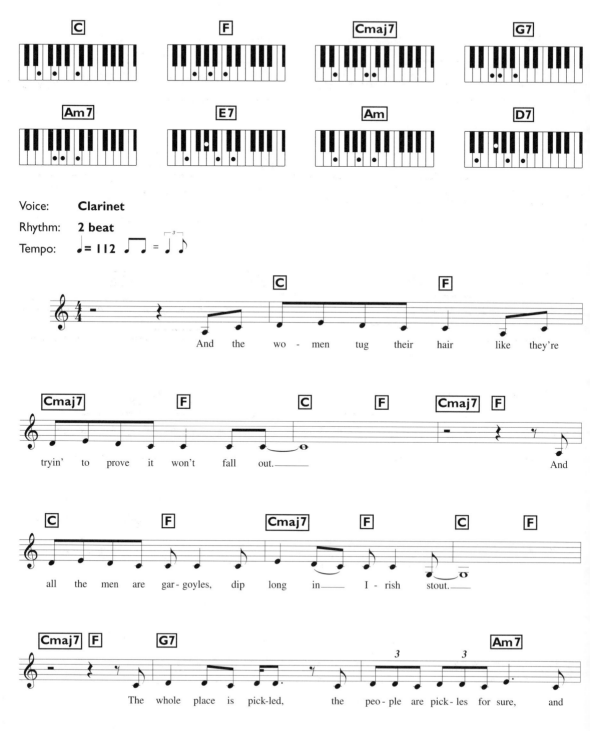

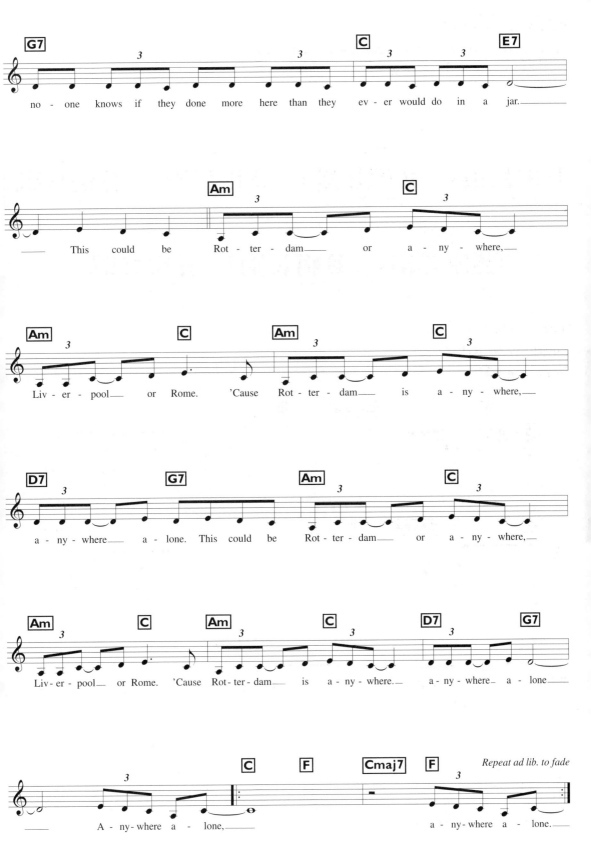

RUNAWAY

Words & Music by Andrea Corr, Caroline Corr, Sharon Corr & Jim Corr
© Copyright 1995 Universal-Songs Of PolyGram International Incorporated/
Beacon Communications Music Company, USA.
Universal Music Publishing Limited, 77 Fulham Palace Road, London W6.
All Rights Reserved. International Copyright Secured.

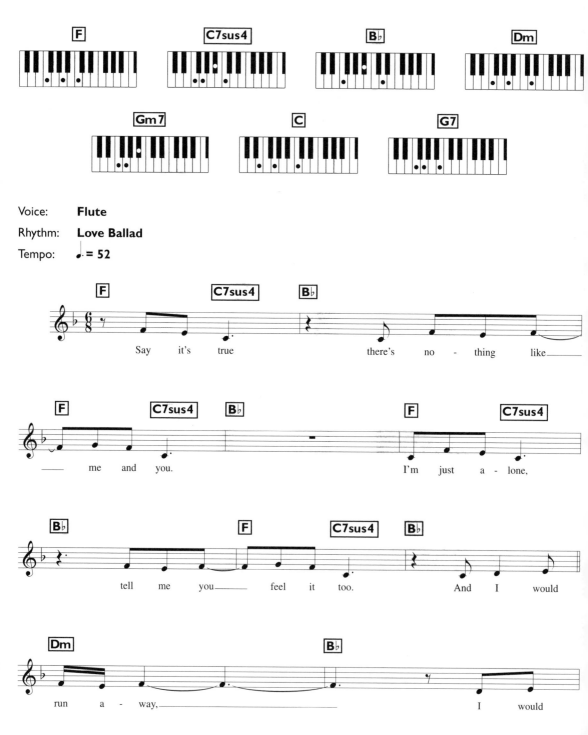

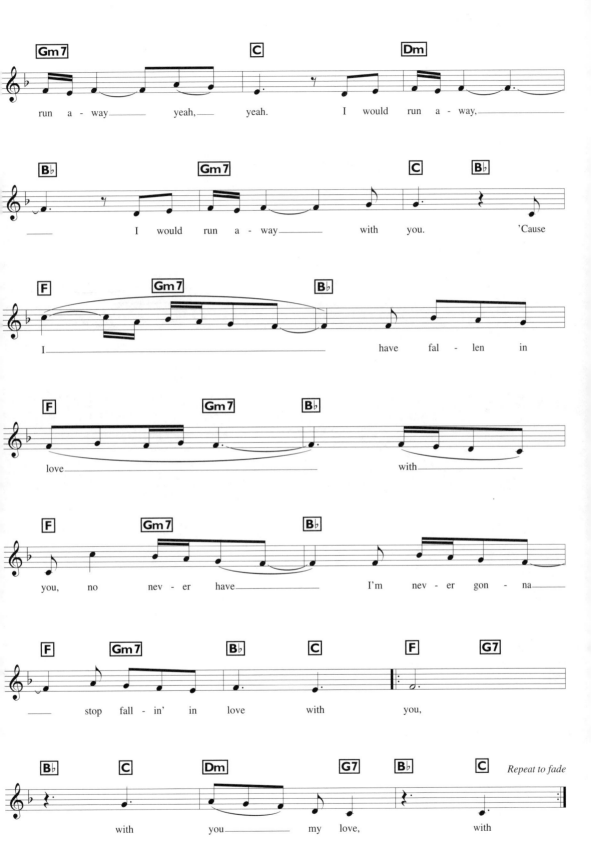

129

SATURDAY NIGHT

Words & Music by Alfredo Pignagnoli & Davide Riva

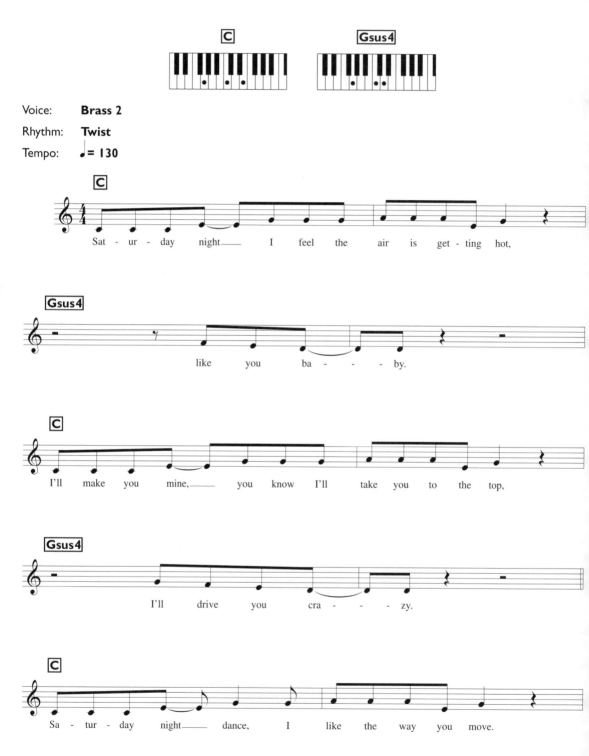

Voice: **Brass 2**

Rhythm: **Twist**

Tempo: ♩ = 130

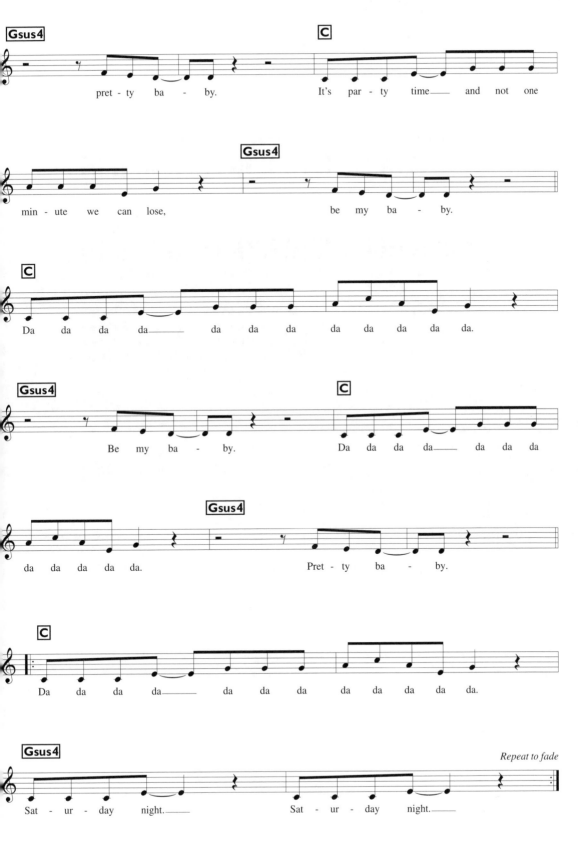

SAY YOU'LL BE THERE

Words & Music by Eliot Kennedy, Jon B. Victoria Aadams, Melanie Brown,
Emma Bunton, Melanie Chisholm & Geri Halliwell

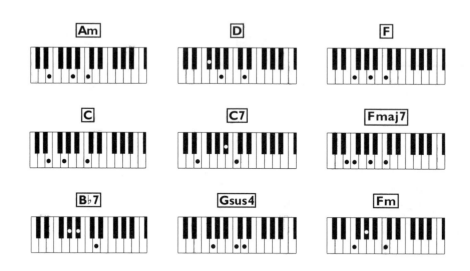

Voice:	**Clarinet**
Rhythm:	**Soul Ballad**
Tempo:	♩ = 108

Last time, that we had this con-ver-sa-tion,

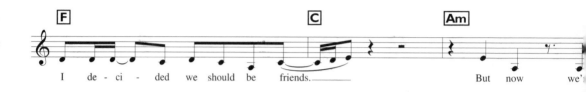

I de-ci-ded we should be friends. But now we'

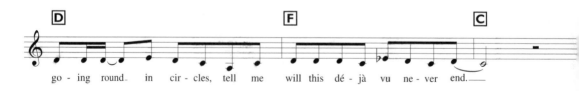

go-ing round in cir-cles, tell me will this dé-jà vu ne-ver end.

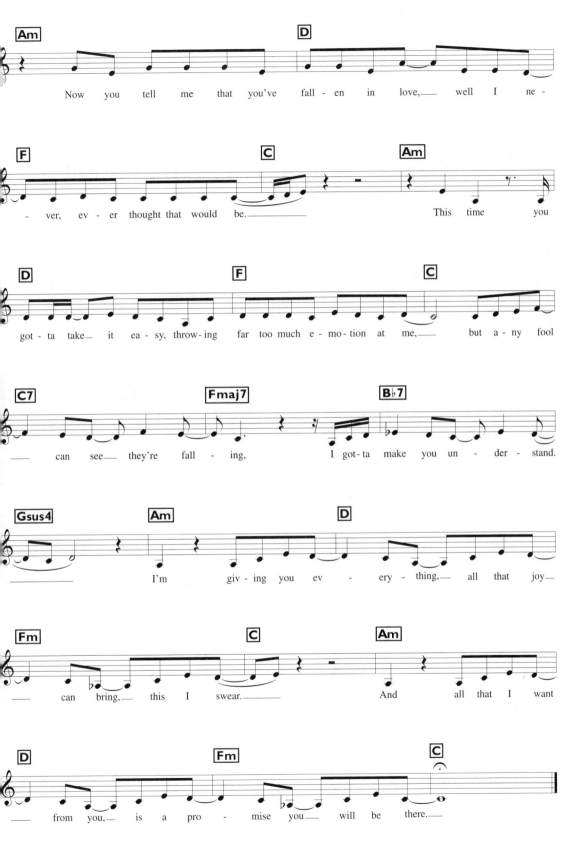

Now you tell me that you've fall-en in love,___ well I ne-ver, ev-er thought that would be.___ This time you got-ta take___ it ea-sy, throw-ing far too much e-mo-tion at me,___ but a-ny fool can see___ they're fall-ing, I got-ta make you un-der-stand. ___ I'm giv-ing you ev-er-y-thing,___ all that joy___ can bring,___ this I swear.___ And all that I want from you,___ is a pro-mise you___ will be there.___

SEARCH FOR THE HERO

Words & Music by Mike Pickering & Paul Heard

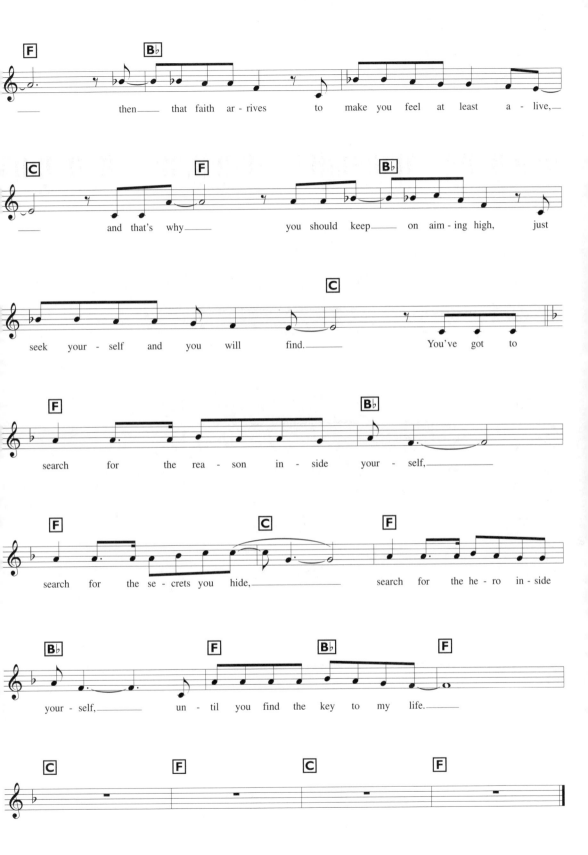

SO YOUNG

Words & Music by Andrea Corr, Caroline Corr, Sharon Corr & Jim Corr

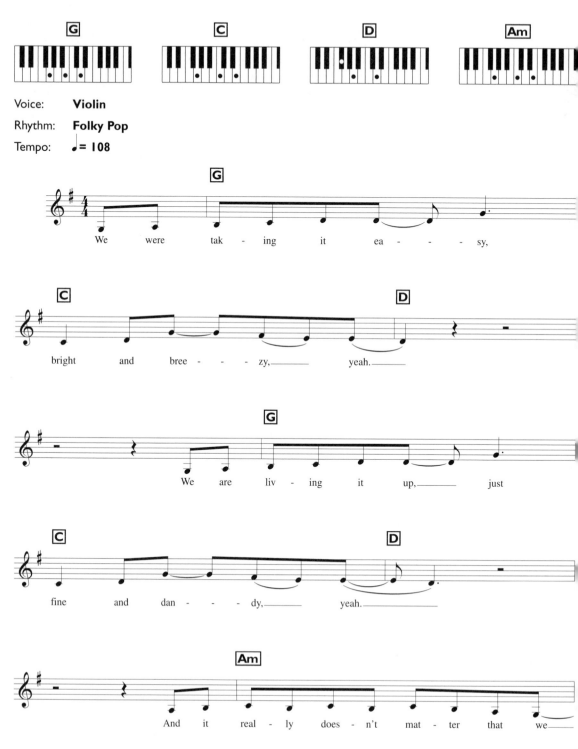

Voice: **Violin**

Rhythm: **Folky Pop**

Tempo: ♩ = 108

We were tak - ing it ea - - sy,

bright and bree - - zy, ___ yeah. ___

We are liv - ing it up, ___ just

fine and dan - - dy, ___ yeah. ___

And it real - ly does - n't mat - ter that we

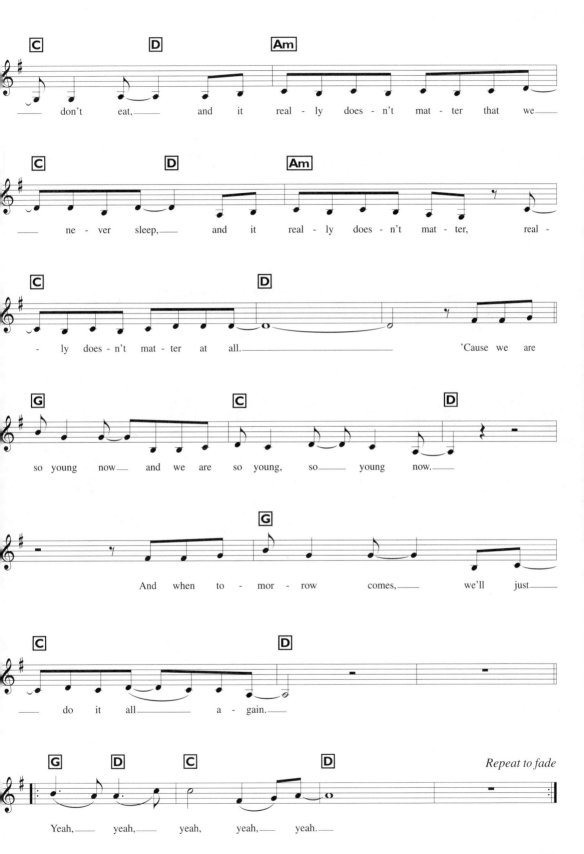

don't eat,___ and it real - ly does - n't mat - ter that we___

ne - ver sleep,___ and it real - ly does - n't mat - ter, real -

- ly does - n't mat - ter at all.___ 'Cause we are

so young now___ and we are so young, so___ young now.___

And when to - mor - row comes,___ we'll just___

___ do it all___ a - gain.___

Yeah,___ yeah,___ yeah, yeah,___ yeah.___

Repeat to fade

SPICE UP YOUR LIFE

Words & Music by Geri Halliwell, Emma Bunton, Melanie Brown, Melanie Chisholm,
Victoria Aadams, Richard Stannard & Matt Rowe

STAY ANOTHER DAY

Words & Music by Tony Mortimer, Robert Kean & Dominic Hawken

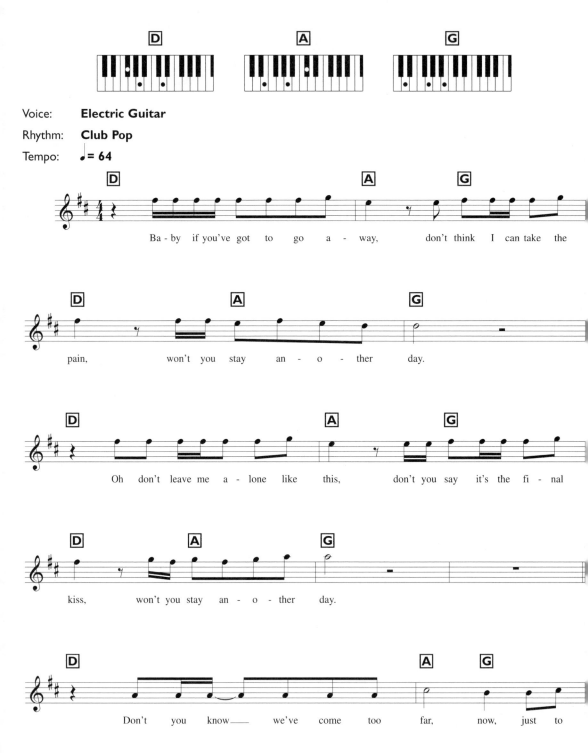

Voice: **Electric Guitar**

Rhythm: **Club Pop**

Tempo: ♩ = **64**

Ba - by if you've got to go a - way, don't think I can take the

pain, won't you stay an - o - ther day.

Oh don't leave me a - lone like this, don't you say it's the fi - nal

kiss, won't you stay an - o - ther day.

Don't you know— we've come too far, now, just to

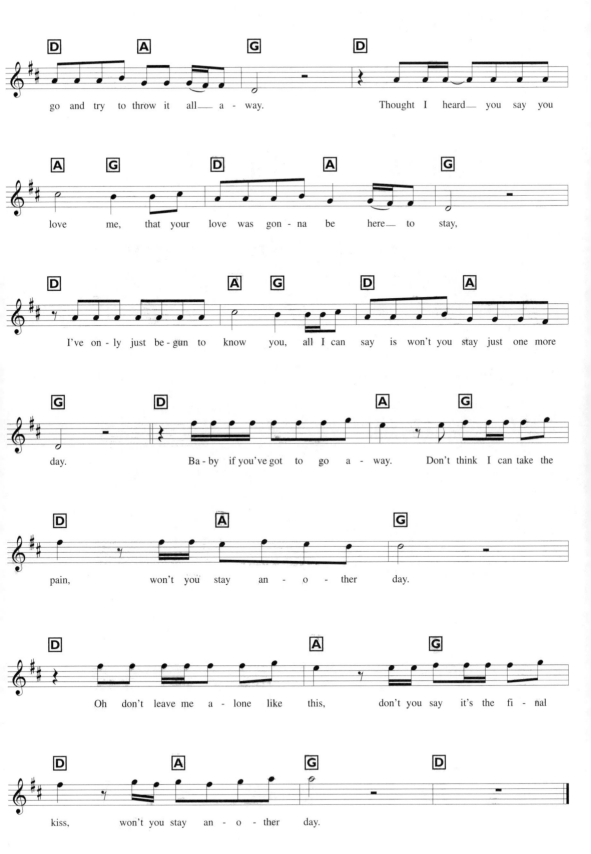

go and try to throw it all— a - way. Thought I heard— you say you

love me, that your love was gon - na be here— to stay,

I've on - ly just be - gun to know you, all I can say is won't you stay just one more

day. Ba - by if you've got to go a - way. Don't think I can take the

pain, won't you stay an - o - ther day.

Oh don't leave me a - lone like this, don't you say it's the fi - nal

kiss, won't you stay an - o - ther day.

TAKE MY BREATH AWAY

Words by Tom Whitlock
Music by Giorgio Moroder

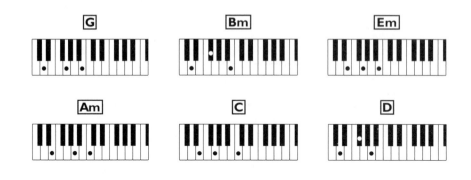

Voice:	**Clarinet**
Rhythm:	**Rock**
Tempo:	**♩ = 96**

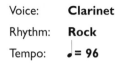

Watch-in' ev-'ry mo-tion in⸺ my fool-ish lov-er's game;⸺

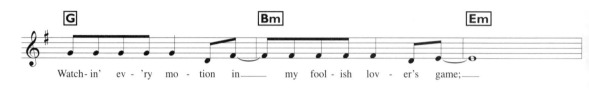

on this end-less o-cean, fi-n'lly lov-ers know no shame.

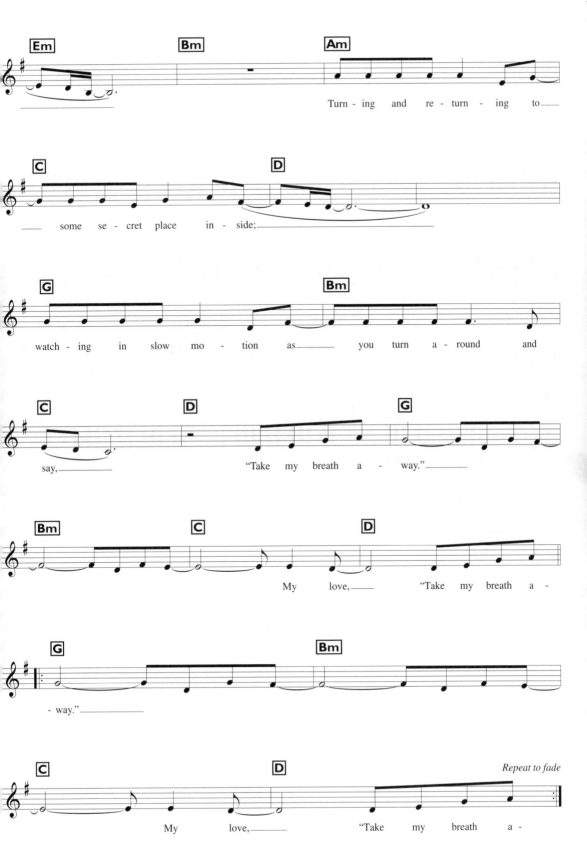

Turn - ing and re - turn - ing to

some se - cret place in - side;

watch - ing in slow mo - tion as you turn a - round and

say, "Take my breath a - way."

My love, "Take my breath a -

- way."

Repeat to fade

My love, "Take my breath a -

TEARS IN HEAVEN

Words & Music by Eric Clapton & Will Jennings
© Copyright 1991 & 1997 E.C. Music Limited, London NW1 (87.5%).
© Copyright 1991 Blue Sky Rider Songs administered by Rondor Music (London) Limited,
10a Parsons Green, London SW6 for the World (excluding USA & Canada) (12.5%).
All Rights Reserved. International Copyright Secured.

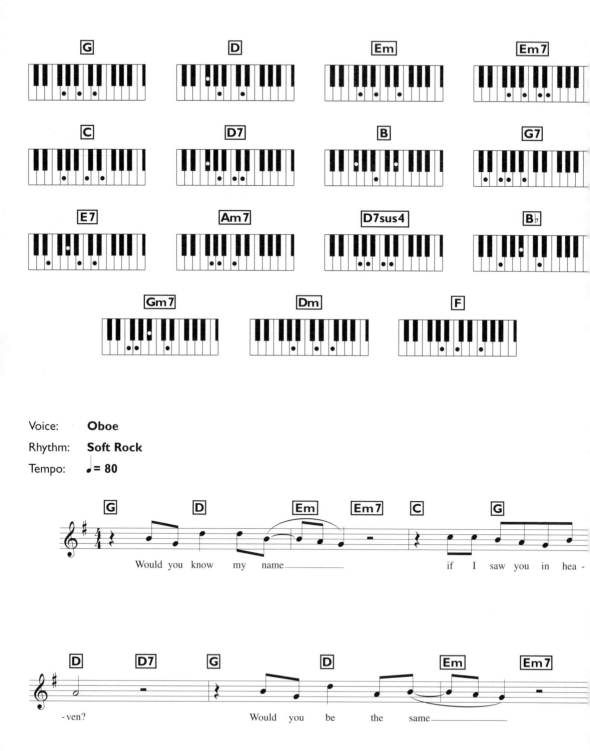

Voice: **Oboe**

Rhythm: **Soft Rock**

Tempo: ♩ = 80

Would you know my name _____ if I saw you in hea-

-ven? Would you be the same _____

if I saw you in hea - ven?   I must be strong

and car - ry on,____ 'cause I know I don't be - long

____ here in hea - ven.

Time can bring you down,____ time can bend your knees.____

Time can break the heart,____ have you beg - ging please,

____ beg - ging please.____

TELL HIM

Words & Music by Linda Thompson, Walter Afanasieff & David Foster

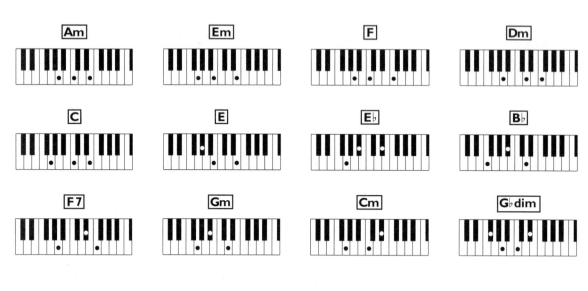

Voice: **Pan Flute**

Rhythm: **Pop Ballad**

Tempo: ♩= 80

I'm   scared,   so a-fraid to   show   I   care.

Will he think me   weak   if I trem-ble when I   speak?

There's an-oth-er   one he's   think-ing of,

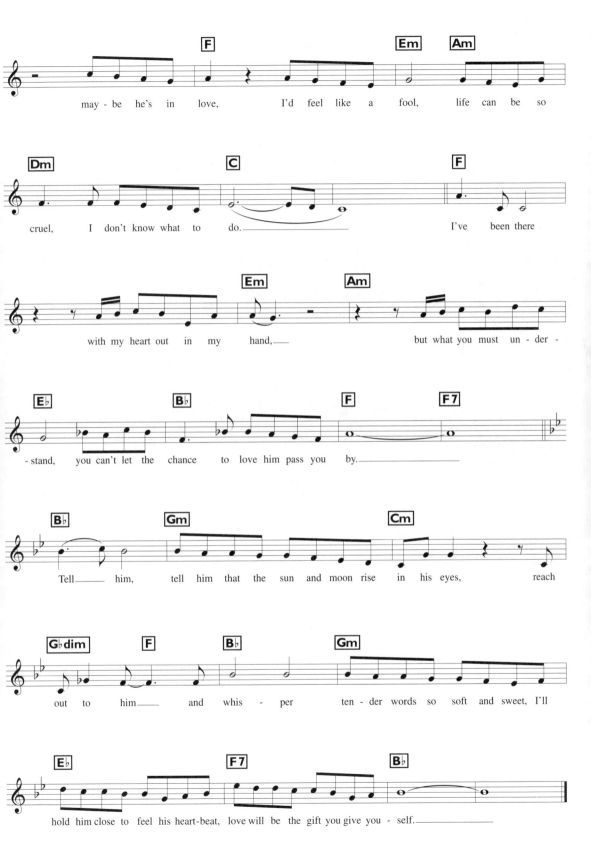

may - be he's in love, I'd feel like a fool, life can be so cruel, I don't know what to do. I've been there with my heart out in my hand, but what you must un - der - stand, you can't let the chance to love him pass you by. Tell him, tell him that the sun and moon rise in his eyes, reach out to him and whis - per ten - der words so soft and sweet, I'll hold him close to feel his heart-beat, love will be the gift you give you - self.

THAT'S THE WAY (I LIKE IT)

Words & Music by Harry Casey & Richard Finch

Voice: **Synth. Bass**

Rhythm: **Funky Pop 1**

Tempo: ♩= 114

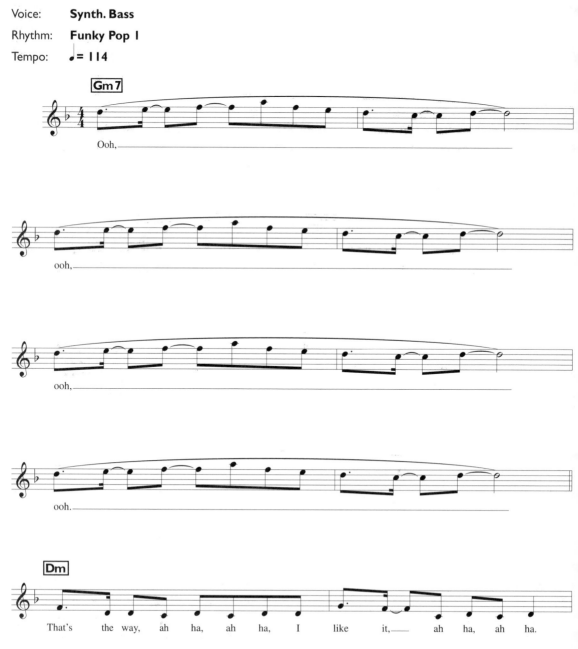

Ooh,

ooh,

ooh,

ooh.

That's the way, ah ha, ah ha, I like it, ah ha, ah ha.

That's the way, ah ha, ah ha, I like it,—— ah ha, ah ha. That's the way, ah ha, ah ha, I

like it,—— ah ha, ah ha. That's the way, ah ha, ah ha, I like it,—— ah ha, ah ha.

Gm7

When you take me—— by the hand, tell me you're my lov - ing

man. Will you give me—— all your love—— and

do it babe, the ve - ry best you can.

Dm

That's the way, ah ha, ah ha, I like it,—— ah ha, ah ha.

Repeat to fade

That's the way, ah ha, ah ha, I like it,—— ah ha, ah ha.

THREE LIONS

Words by David Baddiel & Frank Skinner
Music by Ian Broudie

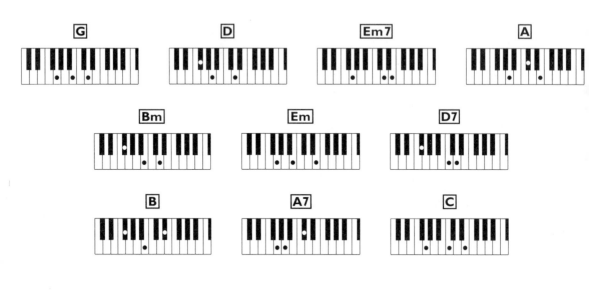

Voice: **Trumpet**

Rhythm: **Slow Rock (2)**

Tempo: ♩ = 126

It's com-ing home,— it's com-ing home,— it's com-ing, foot-ball's com-ing home,

—— it's com-ing home,— it's com-ing home,— it's com-ing, foot-ball's com-ing home,

—— it's com-ing home, it's com-ing home,— it's com-ing, foot-ball's com-ing home.—

TORN

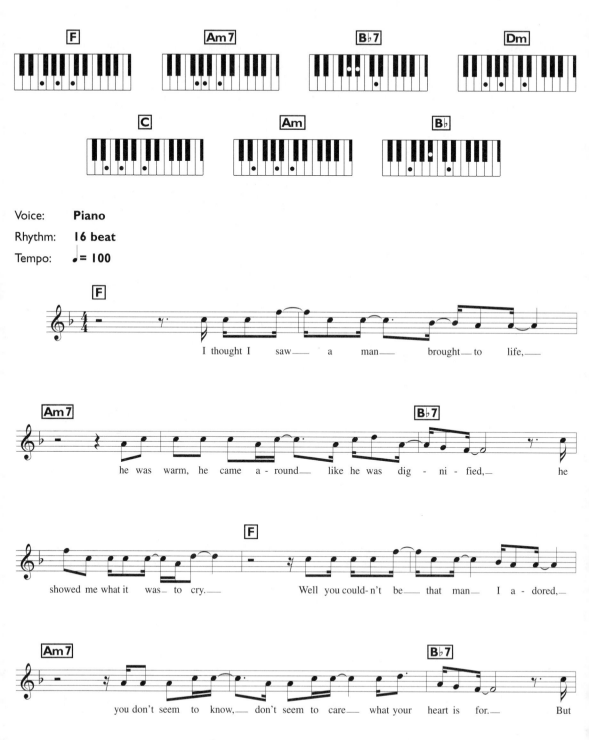

Voice: **Piano**

Rhythm: **16 beat**

Tempo: ♩ = 100

I thought I saw a man brought to life,

he was warm, he came a-round like he was dig-ni-fied, he

showed me what it was to cry. Well you could-n't be that man I a-dored,

you don't seem to know, don't seem to care what your heart is for. But

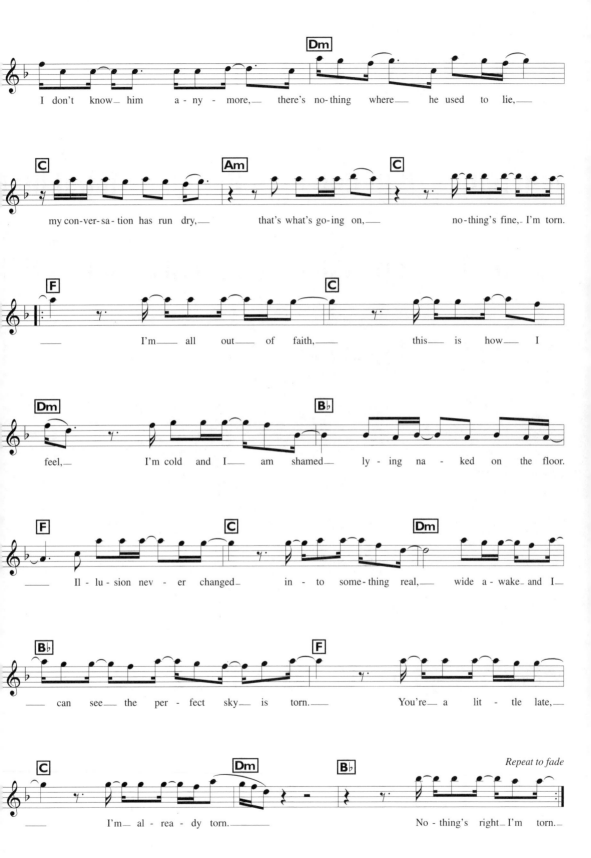

Repeat to fade

TURN BACK TIME

Words & Music by Soren Rasted, Claus Norreen, Johnny Pederson & Karsten Delgado
© Copyright 1997 MCA Music Scandinavia AB & Warner Chappell Music, Denmark.
Universal/MCA Music Limited, 77 Fulham Palace Road, London W6 (91.67%) &
Warner Chappell Music Limited, Griffin House, 161 Hammersmith Road, London W6 (8.33%).
All Rights Reserved. International Copyright Secured.

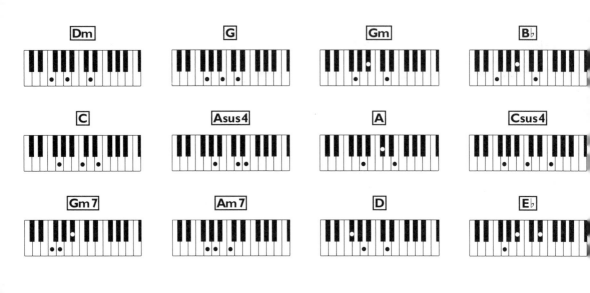

Voice: **French Horn 2**

Rhythm: **Lite Pop**

Tempo: ♩= 108

Give me time to rea - son, give me time to think it through, —

pas - sing through the sea - son where I cheat - ed you. ____

I will al - ways have a cross to wear — but the bolt re-minds me I was there. ____ So

give me— strength— to face this test— of mine.———— If on-ly I could

turn—— back time,——— if on-ly I had said what I— still— hide.—— If on-ly I could

turn—— back time——— I would stay.

The nail re-minds me I was there.

The nail re-minds me I was there. If on-ly I could

turn—— back time,——— if on-ly I had said what I— still— hide.—— If on-ly I could

turn—— back time——— I would stay for the night.—— If on-ly I could

Repeat to fade

2 BECOME 1

Words & Music by Victoria Aadams, Melanie Brown, Emma Bunton,
Melanie Chisholm, Geri Halliwell, Matt Rowe & Richard Stannard

Voice: **Saxophone**

Rhythm: **Soft Rock**

Tempo: ♩ = 72

two be-come one._____ I need some love like I ne-ver need-ed love be - fore, (wan na make love to ya ba-by.) I

had a lit-tle love   now I'm back for more, (wanna make love to ya ba-by.) Set your spi-rit   free,__   it's the

on - ly way   to be._____

Be a lit - tle bit wi - ser ba - by,__

___ (put it on, put it on.)_ 'Cause to - night__   is the   night___   when two be-come one._____ I

need some love like I ne-ver need-ed love be - fore,_(wanna make love to ya ba-by.) I had a lit-tle love, now I'm back for

more, (wan-na make love to ya ba-by.) I need some love like I ne-ver need-ed love be-fore,_(wan-na make love to ya ba-by.) I

had a lit- tle love,   now I'm back for   more,(wanna make love to ya ba-by.) Set your spi-rit   free,__   it's the

Repeat to fade

on - ly way___ to be._____

It's the

157

(UN, DOS, TRES) MARIA

Words & Music by Ian Blake, Luis Gomez Escolar & Karl Porter

Voice: **Clarinet**

Rhythm: **Bossa Nova**

Tempo: ♩ = 132

Un dos tres, un— pa - si - to pa'de - lan - te Ma - ri - a. Un dos tres, un—

— pa - si - to pa' - tras.— Un dos tres, un - pa - si - to pa'de lan - te Ma - ri - a.

Un dos tres, un— pa - si - to pa' - tras.— Un—

— pa - si - to pa - lan - te, un— pa - si - to pa' - tras.— Un

— pa - si - to pa - lan - te, un— pa - si - to pa' - tras.— Un

— pa - si - to pa - lan - te, un— pa - si - to pa' - tras.— Un—

— pa - si - to pa - lan - te, un— pa - si - to pa' - tras.—

UNCHAINED MELODY

Words by Hy Zaret
Music by Alex North

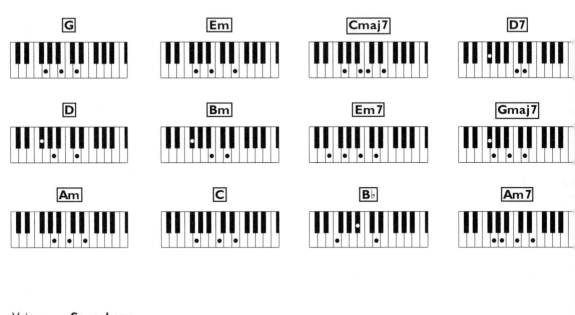

Voice: **Saxophone**

Rhythm: **Ballad**

Tempo: ♩ = 96

Oh my love my dar - ling, I've hun - gered for your

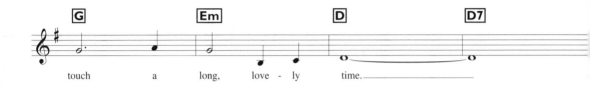

touch a long, love - ly time.

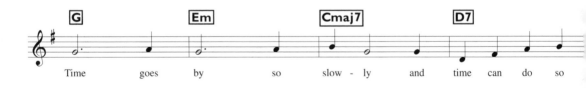

Time goes by so slow - ly and time can do so

much, are you still mine?_____ I need your love,_____

_____ I need your love,_____ God speed your love_____

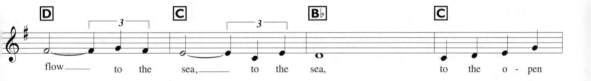

to me!_____ Lone - ly ri - vers

flow_____ to the sea,_____ to the sea, to the o - pen

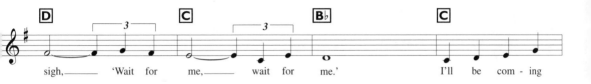

arms_____ of the sea._____ Lone - ly ri - vers

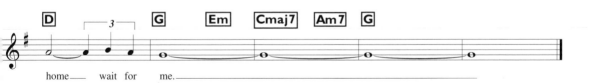

sigh,_____ 'Wait for me,_____ wait for me.' I'll be com - ing

home_____ wait for me._____

161

VIVA FOREVER

Words & Music by Victoria Aadams, Emma Bunton, Melanie Brown,
Melanie Chisholm, Geri Halliwell, Richard Stannard & Matt Rowe
© Copyright 1997 EMI Music Publishing (WP) Limited, 127 Charing Cross Road, London WC2 (50%)/
Universal Music Publishing Limited, 77 Fulham Palace Road, London W6 (50%).
All Rights Reserved. International Copyright Secured.

Voice: **Gut Guitar**

Rhythm: **Pop Ballad**

Tempo: ♩ = 84

Do you still re-mem-ber how we used to be?

Feel-ing to-geth-er, be-liev-ing what-ev-er, my love has said to me.

Both of us were dream-ers, young love in the sun,

felt like my sav-iour, my spi-rit I gave you, we'd on-ly just be-gan.

Has-ta ma-ña-na, al-ways be mine. Vi-va for-ev-

- er,_____ I'll be wait - ing,_____ ev - er - last -

- ing_____ like the sun._____ Live for - ev -

- er,_____ for the mo - ment,_____ ev - er search -

- ing_____ for the one._____ Vi - va for - ev -

- er,_____ I'll be wait - ing,_____ ev - er - last - ing_____ like the sun..

_____ Live for - ev - er,_____ for the mo - ment,_____ ev - er search-

- ing_____ for the one._____

WALKING ON SUNSHINE

Words & Music by Kimberley Rew

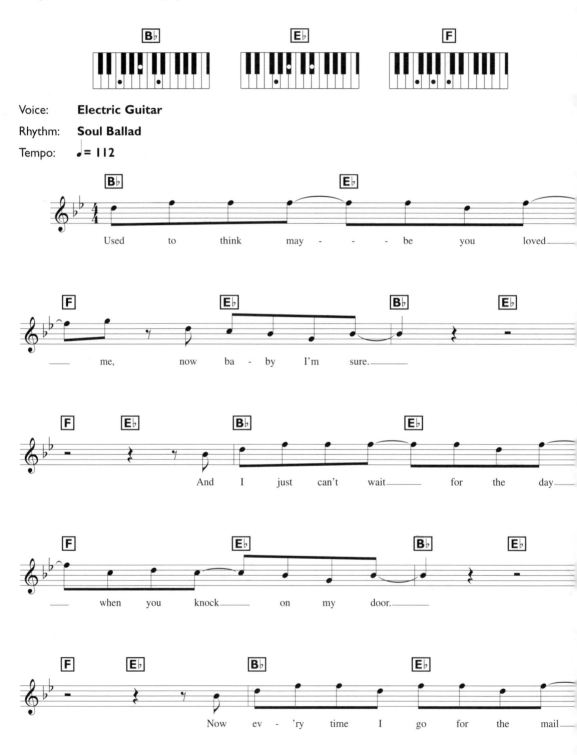

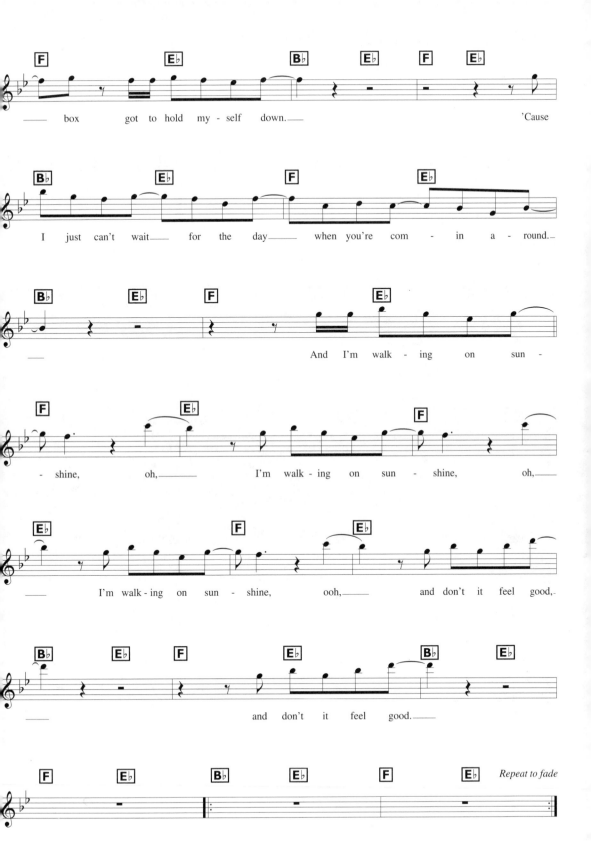

WHAT CAN I DO

Words & Music by Andrea Corr, Caroline Corr, Sharon Corr & Jim Corr

Voice: **Alto Saxophone**

Rhythm: **Folksy Pop**

Tempo: ♩ = 80

I have-n't slept at all in days,

it's been so long since we have talked.

And I have been here ma - ny times,

I just don't know what I'm do - in' wrong.

What can I do to make you love me?

167

WHEN YOU TELL ME THAT YOU LOVE ME

Words & Music by Albert Hammond & John Bettis

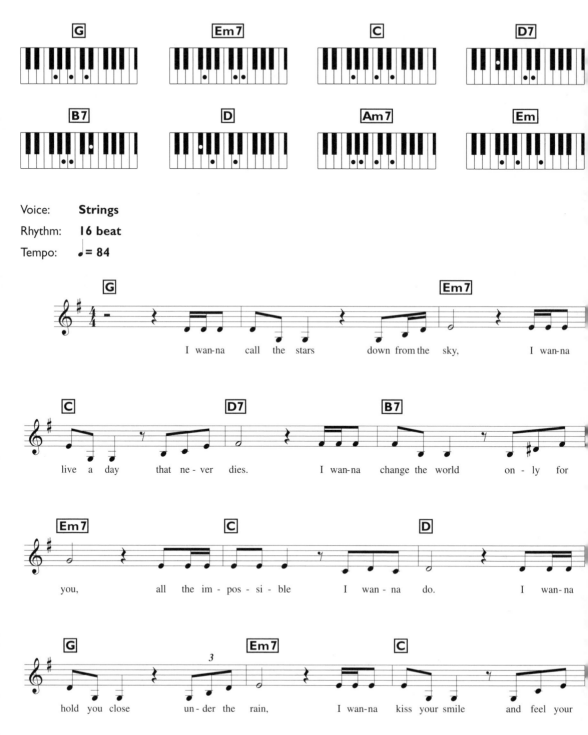

Voice: **Strings**

Rhythm: **16 beat**

Tempo: ♩ = 84

I wan-na call the stars down from the sky, I wan-na live a day that ne-ver dies. I wan-na change the world on-ly for you, all the im-pos-si-ble I wan-na do. I wan-na hold you close un-der the rain, I wan-na kiss your smile and feel your

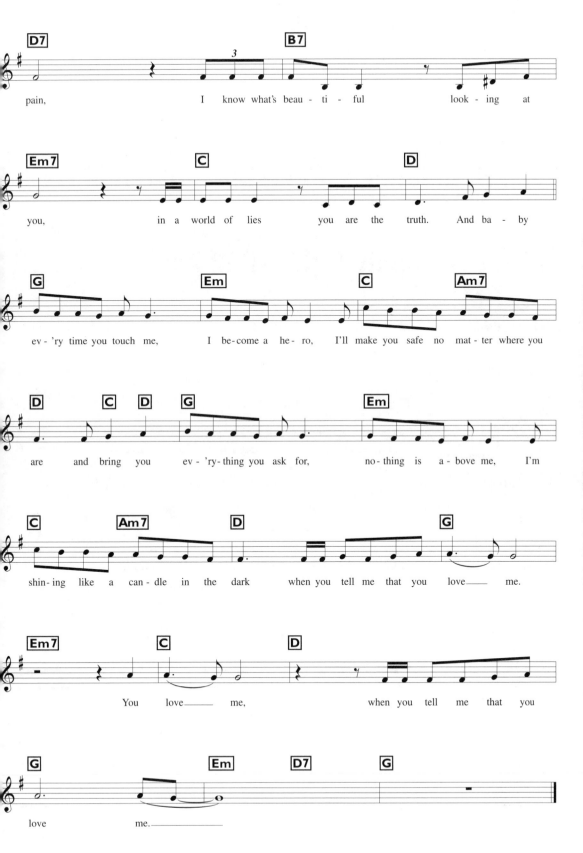

pain, I know what's beau - ti - ful look - ing at

you, in a world of lies you are the truth. And ba - by

ev - 'ry time you touch me, I be - come a he - ro, I'll make you safe no mat - ter where you

are and bring you ev - 'ry - thing you ask for, no - thing is a - bove me, I'm

shin - ing like a can - dle in the dark when you tell me that you love____ me.

You love____ me, when you tell me that you

love me.____

WHEN YOU'RE GONE

Words & Music by Bryan Adams & Eliot Kennedy

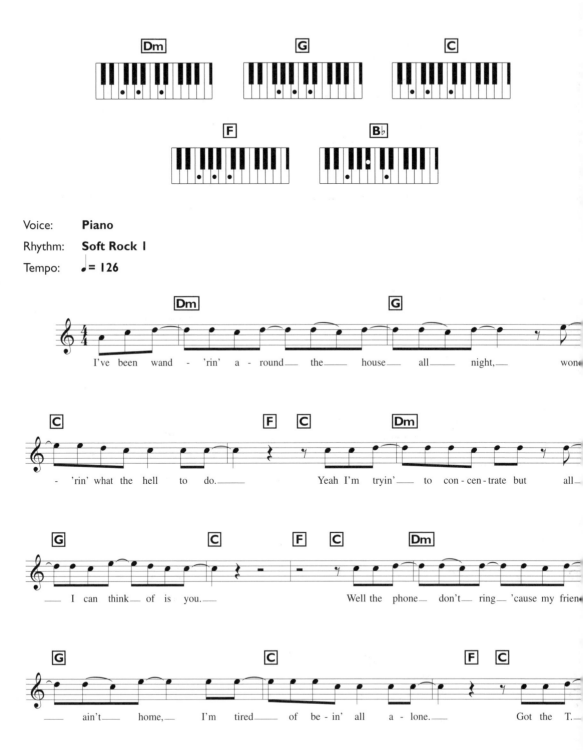

Voice: **Piano**

Rhythm: **Soft Rock 1**

Tempo: ♩ = 126

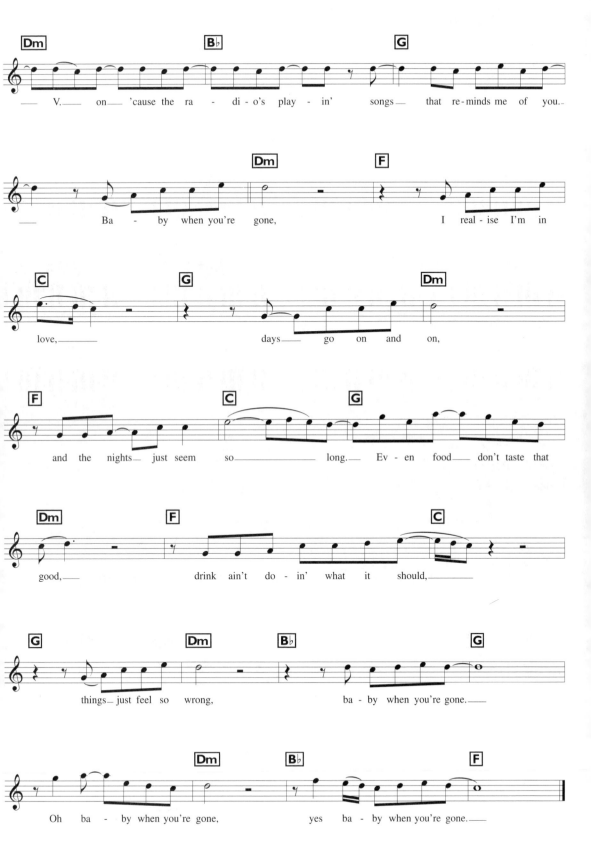

A WHOLE NEW WORLD
(From Walt Disney Pictures' "Aladdin")

Music by Alan Menken
Lyrics by Tim Rice

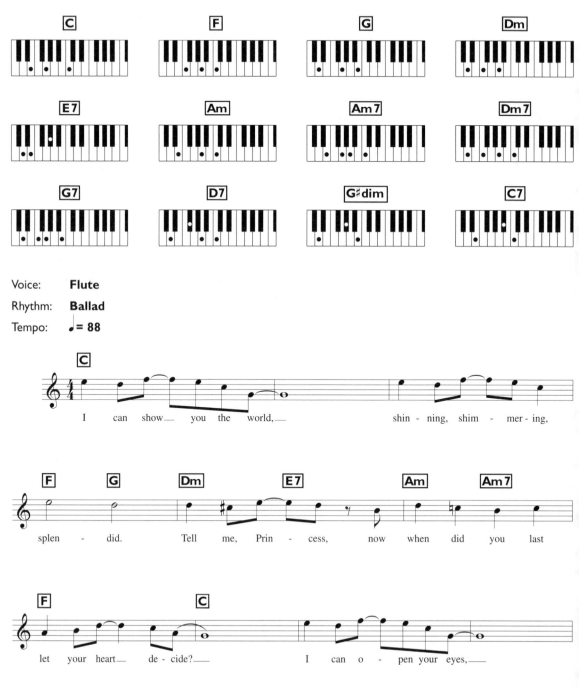

WILD WOOD

Words & Music by Paul Weller

WITHOUT YOU

Words & Music by Peter Ham & Tom Evans
© Copyright 1970 Apple Publishing Limited.
Warner Chappell Music Limited, Griffin House, 161 Hammersmith Road, London W6.
All Rights Reserved. International Copyright Secured.

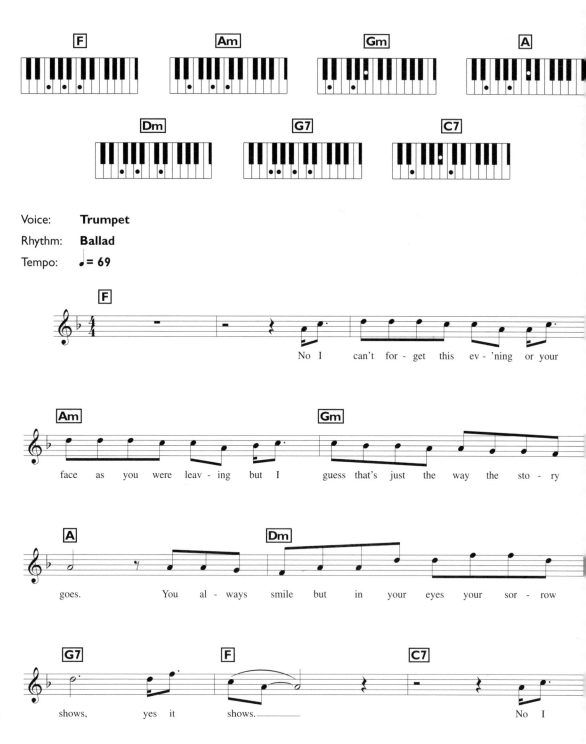

Voice: **Trumpet**

Rhythm: **Ballad**

Tempo: ♩ = 69

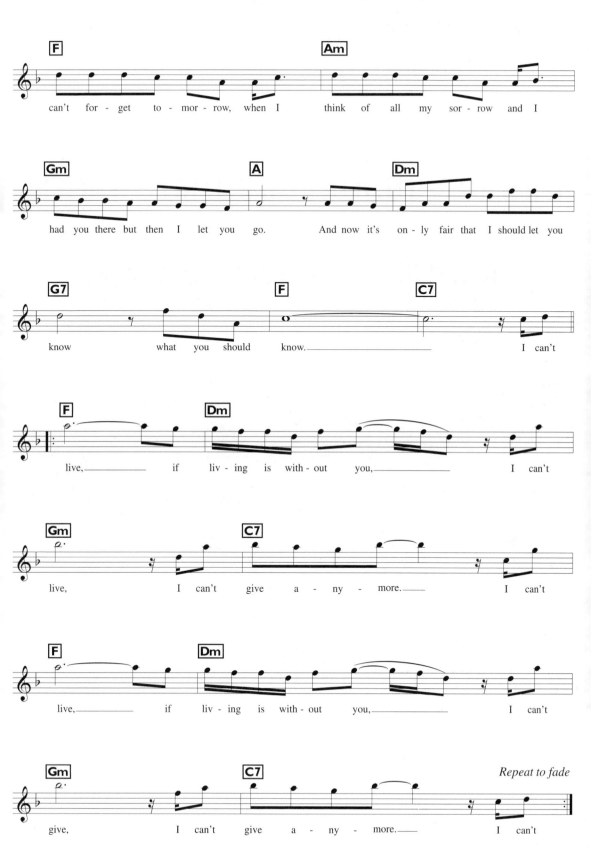

177

WONDERFUL TONIGHT

Words & Music by Eric Clapton
© Copyright 1977 & 1999 Eric Clapton.
All Rights Reserved. International Copyright Secured.

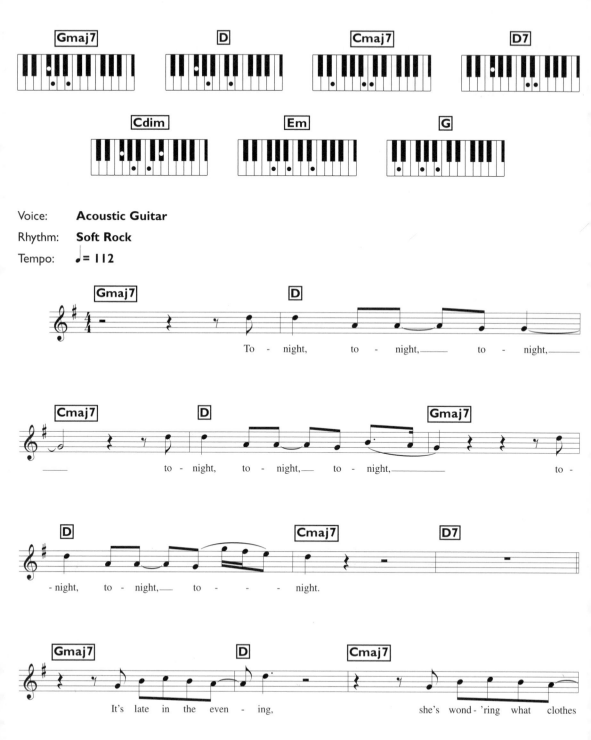

Voice: **Acoustic Guitar**

Rhythm: **Soft Rock**

Tempo: ♩ = 112

Tonight, to - night,____ to - night,____ to - night, to - night,____ to - night,____ to -

- night, to - night,____ to - - night.

It's late in the even - ing, she's wond - 'ring what clothes

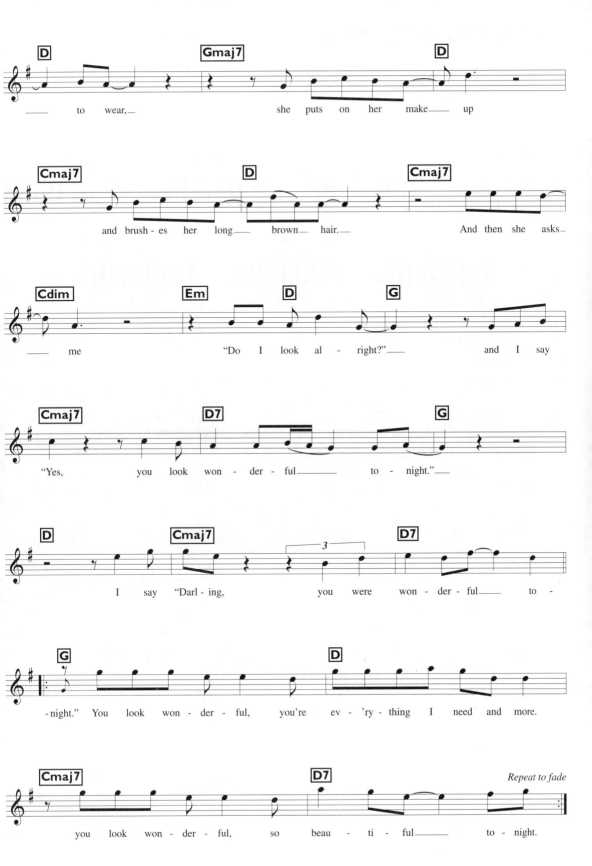

WONDERWALL

Words & Music by Noel Gallagher
© Copyright 1995 Oasis Music, Creation Songs Limited &
Sony/ATV Music Publishing (UK) Limited, 10 Great Marlborough Street, London W1.
All Rights Reserved. International Copyright Secured.

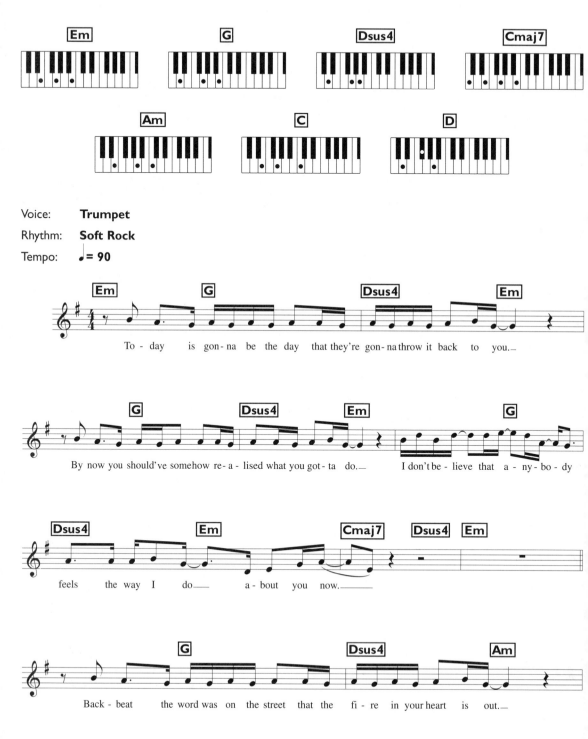

Voice: **Trumpet**

Rhythm: **Soft Rock**

Tempo: ♩ = **90**

I'm sure you've heard it all be-fore, but you ne-ver real-ly had a doubt.

I don't be-lieve that a-ny-bo-dy feels the way I do a-bout you now.

And all the roads we have to walk are wind-

-ing, and all the lights that lead us there are blind-ing.

There are ma-ny things that I would like to say to you, but I don't know how.

I said may-be, you're gon-na be the one that

saves me.

WORDS

Words & Music by Barry Gibb, Robin Gibb & Maurice Gibb

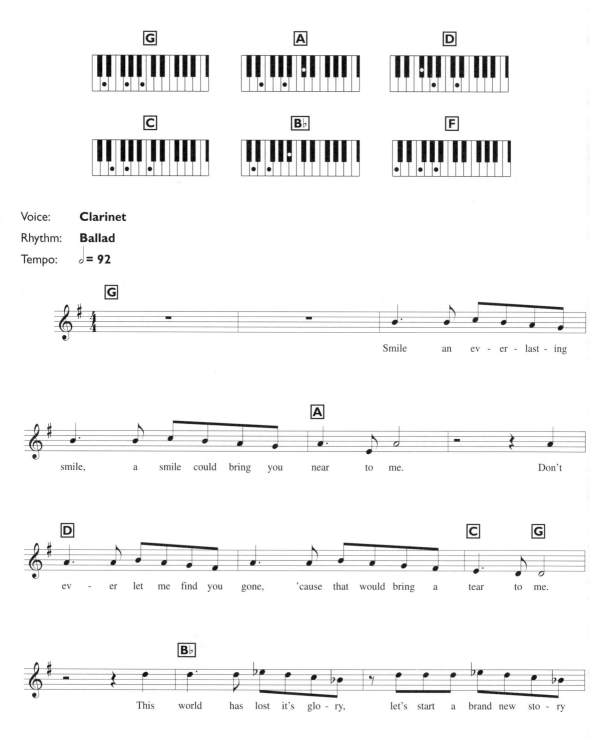

now, my love. Right now, there'll be no oth-er time and I can show you how, my

love.— Talk in ev-er-last-ing words and de-di-cate them all to me.

And I will give you all my life, I'm here if you should call to me.

You think that I don't ev-en mean a sin-gle word I say.

It's on-ly words, and words are all I have to take your heart a-way.

It's on-ly words, and words are all I have to take your heart a-way.

It's on-ly words, and words are all I have to take your heart a-way.

YOU GOTTA BE

Lyrics & Melody by Des'ree
Music by Ashley Ingram

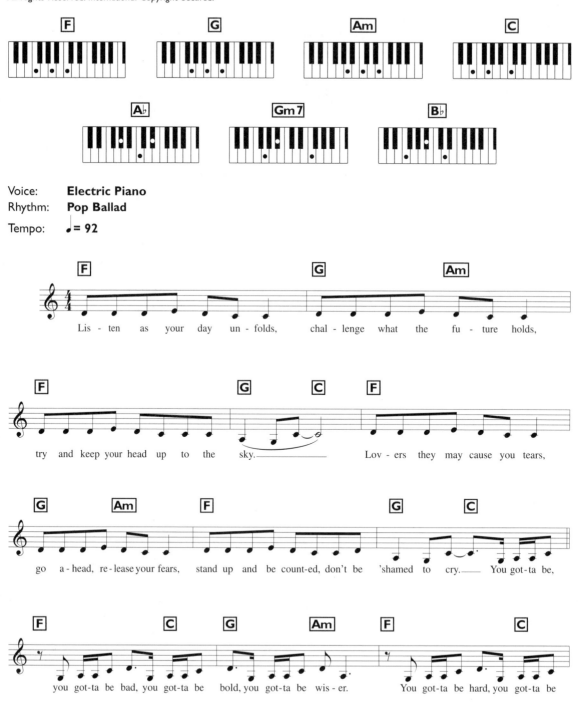

Voice: **Electric Piano**
Rhythm: **Pop Ballad**
Tempo: ♩ = 92

Lis - ten as your day un - folds, chal - lenge what the fu - ture holds,

try and keep your head up to the sky. Lov - ers they may cause you tears,

go a - head, re - lease your fears, stand up and be count - ed, don't be 'shamed to cry. You got - ta be,

you got - ta be bad, you got - ta be bold, you got - ta be wis - er. You got - ta be hard, you got - ta be

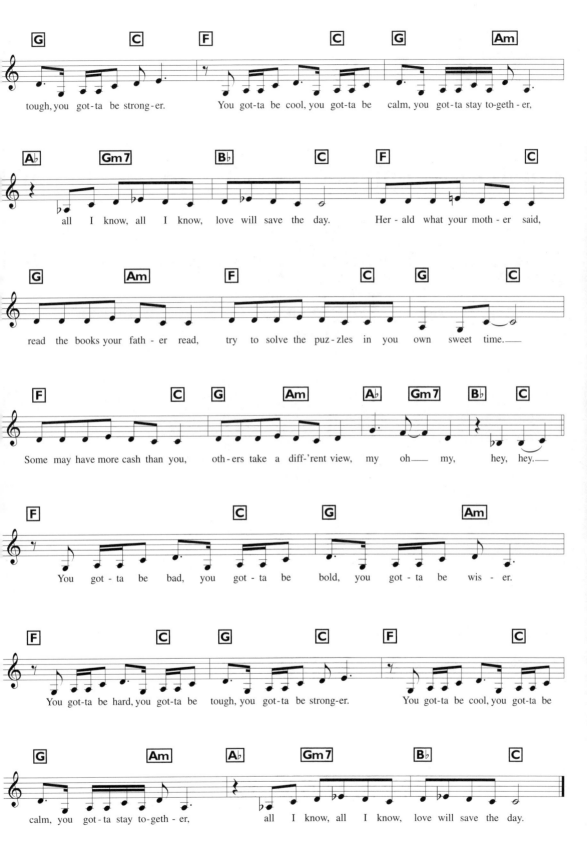

YOU MUST LOVE ME

Music by Andrew Lloyd Webber
Lyrics by Tim Rice

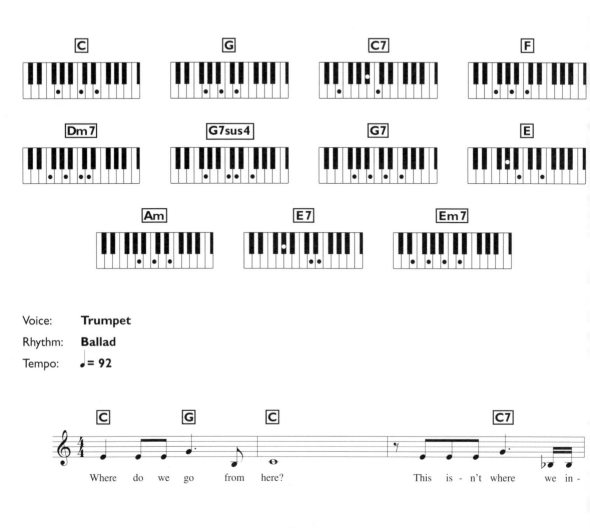

Voice: **Trumpet**
Rhythm: **Ballad**
Tempo: ♩ = 92

Where do we go from here? This is - n't where we in -

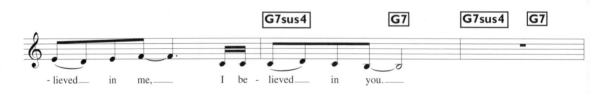

- ten - ded to be. We had it all, you be -

- lieved in me, I be - lieved in you.

YOU'RE STILL THE ONE

Words & Music by Shania Twain & R.J. Lange

© Copyright 1997 Out Of Pocket Productions Limited & Loon Echo Incorporated/
Songs Of PolyGram International Incorporated, USA.
Zomba Music Publishers Limited, 165-167 High Road, London NW10 (40%)/
Universal Music Publishing Limited, 77 Fulham Palace Road, London W6 (60%).
All Rights Reserved. International Copyright Secured.

Voice: **Saxophone**

Rhythm: **Soul Ballad**

Tempo: ♩ = 138

Looks like we made it, look how far we've come my ba - by. We might have took the long way, we knew we'd get there some day. They said, I bet, they'll nev - er make it, but just look at us hold - - ing on,

we're still to-geth-er, still go-ing____ strong.

____ (Still the one) You're still the one I run____ to,____

the one that I be-long____ to.____ You're still the one I want____ for

life. (Still the one) You're still the one that I____ love,____

the on-ly one I dream____ of.____ You're still the one I kiss____ good-

-night. I'm so glad we made____ it,____

look how far____ we've come my ba-by.____

YOUNG AT HEART

Words & Music by Robert Hodgens, Siobhan Fahey,
Keren Woodward & Sarah Dallin

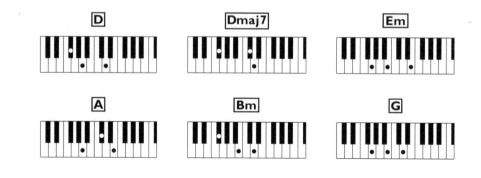

Voice: **Electric Piano 2**

Rhythm: **8 Beat Pop**

Tempo: ♩ = 124

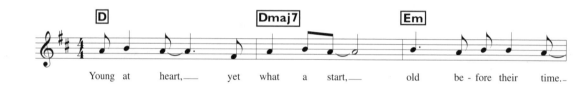

Young at heart, ___ yet what a start, ___ old be - fore their time. ___

___ They mar - ried young ___ for love at last ___

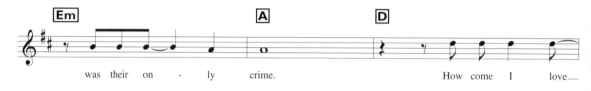

was their on - ly crime. How come I love ___

___ them ___ now, ___ how come I love them more?

190

Exclusive Distributors:

Music Sales Limited
8/9 Frith Street,
London W1V 5TZ, England.

Music Sales Pty Limited
120 Rothschild Avenue,
Rosebery, NSW 2018,
Australia.

Order No. AM962203
ISBN 0-7119-7995-2
This book © Copyright 2000 by Wise Publications
in association with Omnibus Press

Book designed by Chloë Alexander
Compiled by Nick Crispin
Music arranged by Roger Day and Derek Jones
Music processed by Paul Ewers Music Design
Back cover photographs courtesy of LFI/All Action

Printed in the United Kingdom by
Redwood Books Ltd, Trowbridge Wilts

Your Guarantee of Quality
As publishers, we strive to produce every book to the
highest commercial standards. This book has been
carefully designed to minimise awkward page turns and
to make playing from it a real pleasure.
　　Particular care has been given to specifying acid-free,
neutral-sized paper made from pulps which have not
been elemental chlorine bleached. This pulp is from
farmed sustainable forests and was produced with special
regard for the environment.
　　Throughout, the printing and binding have been
planned to ensure a sturdy, attractive publication which
should give years of enjoyment. If your copy fails to meet
our high standards, please inform us and we will gladly
replace it.

Music Sales' complete catalogue describes thousands
of titles and is available in full colour sections by subject,
direct from Music Sales Limited. Please state your areas
of interest and send a cheque/postal order for £1.50 for
postage to: Music Sales Limited, Newmarket Road,
Bury St. Edmunds, Suffolk IP33 3YB.

www.musicsales.com
www.omnibuspress.com